THEN & NOW®

BLACK MOUNTAIN

Anne Chesky Smith

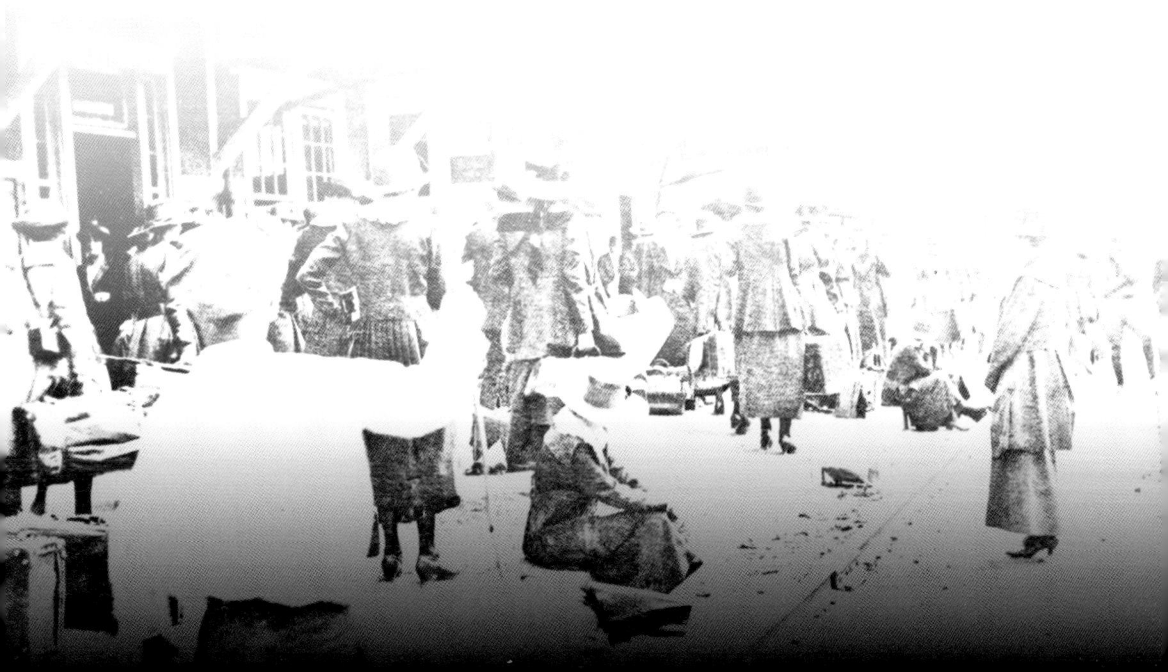

To my family.

ISBN 978-1-4671-2888-9

Library of Congress Control Number: 2018932489

Published by Arcadia Publishing
Charleston, South Carolina

Printed in the United States of America

Then and Now is a registered trademark and is used under license from
Salamander Books Limited

For all general information, please contact Arcadia Publishing:
Telephone 843-853-2070
Fax 843-853-0044
E-mail sales@arcadiapublishing.com
For customer service and orders:
Toll-Free 1-888-313-2665

Visit us on the Internet at www.arcadiapublishing.com

ON THE FRONT COVER: Believed to have been taken during the blizzard that swept across Black Mountain and Western North Carolina on March 17, 1936, this historic photograph shows Rexall Drugs, now Town Hardware and General Store, at the corner of Broadway Avenue and State Street in downtown Black Mountain. In places, snow drifts reached up to eight feet high during the storm. The building was originally built as a drugstore by Dr. Clifford Porter in the late 1920s and had a large marble soda fountain. (Then, courtesy of Swannanoa Valley Museum & History Center; now photograph by the author.)

ON THE BACK COVER: A passenger train arrives at the Black Mountain Depot around 1920. With trains arriving and departing multiple times a day, this area became the commercial center of town. At this time, establishments along what is now Sutton Avenue included a drugstore and boardinghouse, as well as The People's Bank and New York Café. (Courtesy of Swannanoa Valley Museum & History Center.)

Contents

Acknowledgments

This book could not have been written without the previous work done by Joyce Justus Parris in her 1992 publication, *A History of Black Mountain and Its People*, as well as the work of those who compiled the Black Mountain Downtown Historic District National Register nomination. These works provided an important starting place for further research into the photographs, locations, and people featured in this book. Whenever possible, I used primary documentation from the Buncombe County Register of Deeds, newspapers.com (Asheville publications were particularly helpful), and resources available in the Swannanoa Valley Museum & History Center's archives to verify and add to what has already been written in these publications. Another book I found particularly helpful was Joan and Robert Goodson's 1997 *On the North Fork of the Swannanoa River 1880–1950*. Due to limited space, I could not, unfortunately, include every site of importance within Black Mountain, which has a wealth of wonderful historic spaces. Unless otherwise stated, all then images are from the Swannanoa Valley Museum & History Center's archive, and all now images were taken by the author during the latter half of 2017 and beginning of 2018.

Introduction

Used by Native Americans for thousands of years, the mountains of Western North Carolina opened to white settlement after the Revolutionary War. A stagecoach road that eventually became part of the Western Turnpike led through the center of what is now the town of Black Mountain, debarking passengers at the present-day location of the Town Square. This thoroughfare (now State Street) served as the center of development for the town until the coming of the railroad in 1880. Originally known as Grey Eagle, the town changed its name when officially chartered in 1893 to match the name given to the new railroad station, Black Mountain.

Though already a destination for tourists due to its cool climate and proximity to Mount Mitchell, the highest peak in the eastern United States, the arrival of the railroad not only shifted the town's development to the station, it also shifted the economy to focus more on tourism (and extractive industries). Some residents opened their homes to summer boarders, while others built large hotels, inns, restaurants, mercantile stores, and the like to accommodate the growing tourism industry. The mountainous terrain and climate also attracted tuberculosis sanatoriums and religious retreat centers. The summer of 1912 saw around 600 visitors, close to double the town's population. Many visitors stayed and established businesses. Development companies began to plat and market the area for residential neighborhoods.

A major fire in the winter of 1912 destroyed many of the buildings surrounding the depot, and development began to migrate north of the tracks up Cherry Street. By 1916, the roads surrounding the railroad station had been paved—the first municipality in the county to vote to do this—and as the automobile became a more popular option for travel, development of the town shifted back to the original stagecoach road. Most of the buildings still standing along State Street were erected in the 1920s, including a firehouse and town hall.

Black Mountain was not immune to the effects of the Depression, but government programs allowed some growth, most notably the construction of the Lake Tomahawk recreation center. The end of World War II signaled a resurgence of development and simultaneous road improvements, allowing easier travel to Black Mountain. Today, Black Mountain continues to attract tourists who come to the town for its beauty, outdoor recreation, music, shops, restaurants, galleries, museums, Christian assemblies, and general small-town appeal.

CHAPTER 1

Around the Depot

Sutton and Black Mountain Avenues

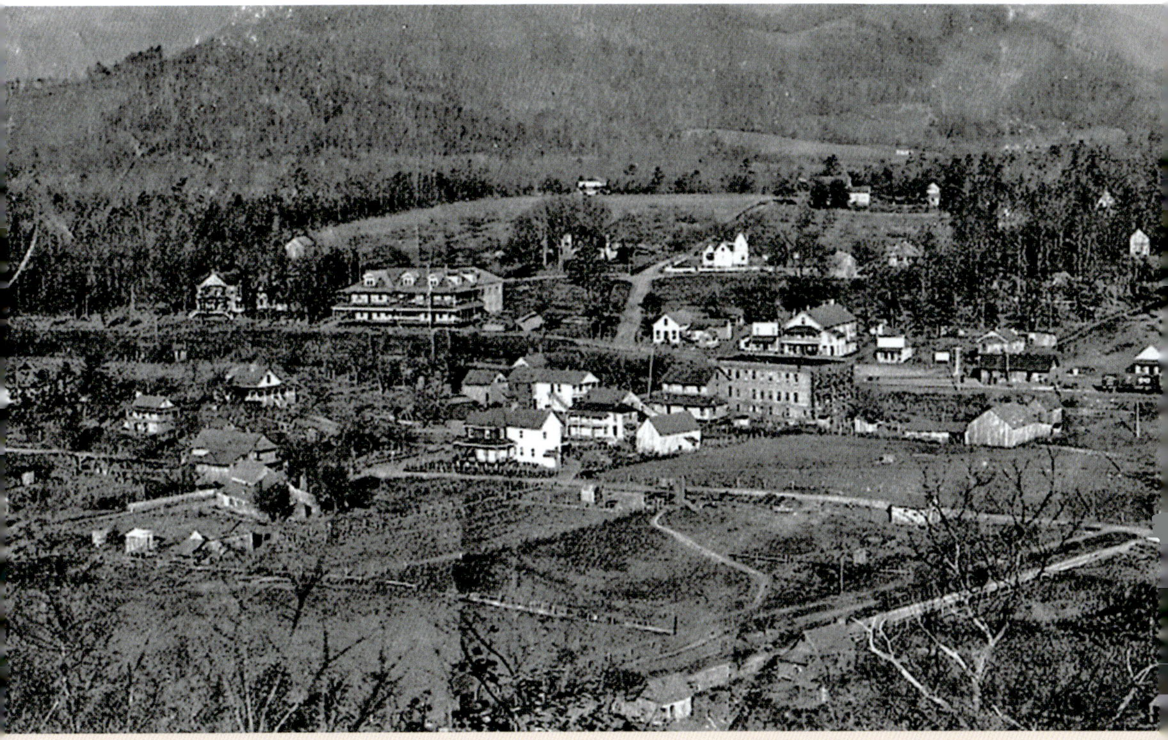

Originally, Black Mountain centered around the stagecoach route (now State Street). Once the railroad established a station in 1880 on Depot Street (now Sutton Avenue), the town's center shifted. This c. 1908 photograph was taken looking northwest. In November 1912, a major fire "practically destroyed the business section of Black Mountain," according to the *Asheville Gazette-News*. Businesses destroyed included the Yates & McGuire grocery, Brown Brothers livery stable, Black Mountain Lumber Company, Carolina Feed & Ice Store, J.S. Wahab dry goods store, Knights of Pythias and Odd Fellows halls, Pemberton & Company's hardware store, Ernest Walker's blacksmith shop, Southern Railway freight depot, and J.I. Bradham's livery stable and furniture store, where the fire started.

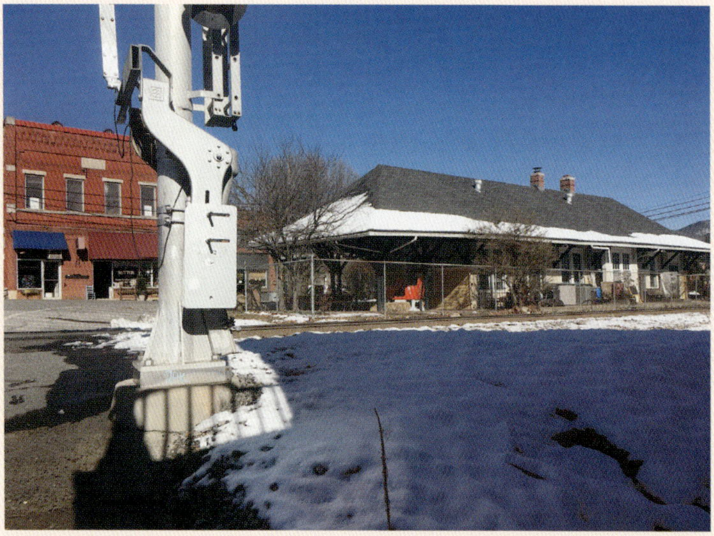

Photographer Gertrude Sprague captured Black Mountain's first train depot as it appeared from south of the tracks prior to 1890. At this time, the depot may have also served as a store and post office. The depot was first rebuilt in 1898. In 1909, Southern Railway rebuilt the depot again, and that building still stands beside the tracks today. Though passenger service to Black Mountain ended in 1975, trains still pass through Black Mountain daily, typically carrying coal to the east and wood chips to the west. Today, the Old Depot Association maintains the depot as an arts and crafts gallery.

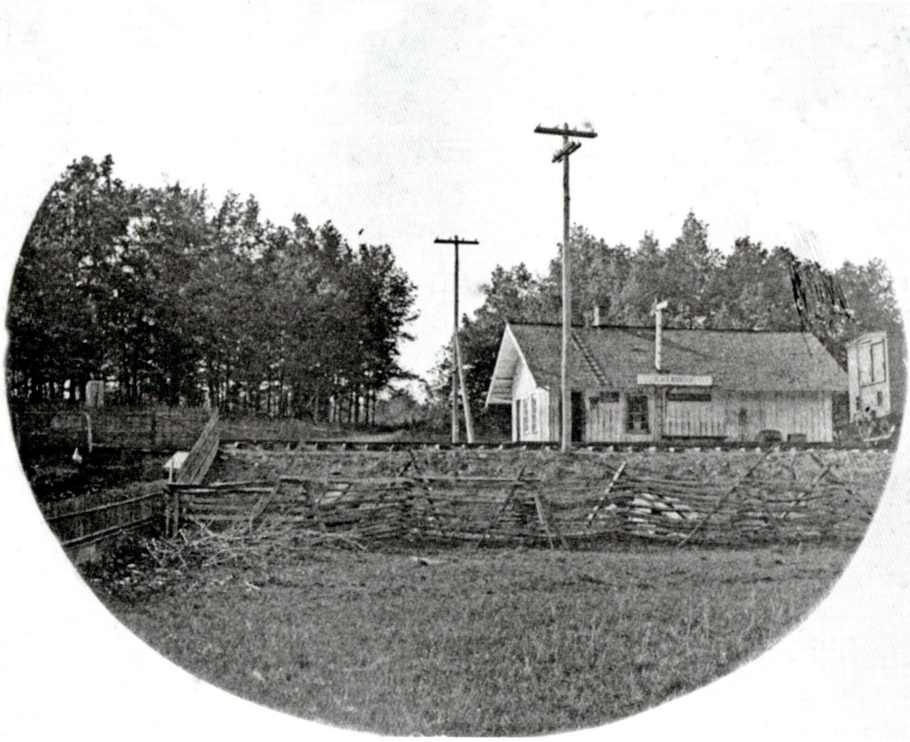

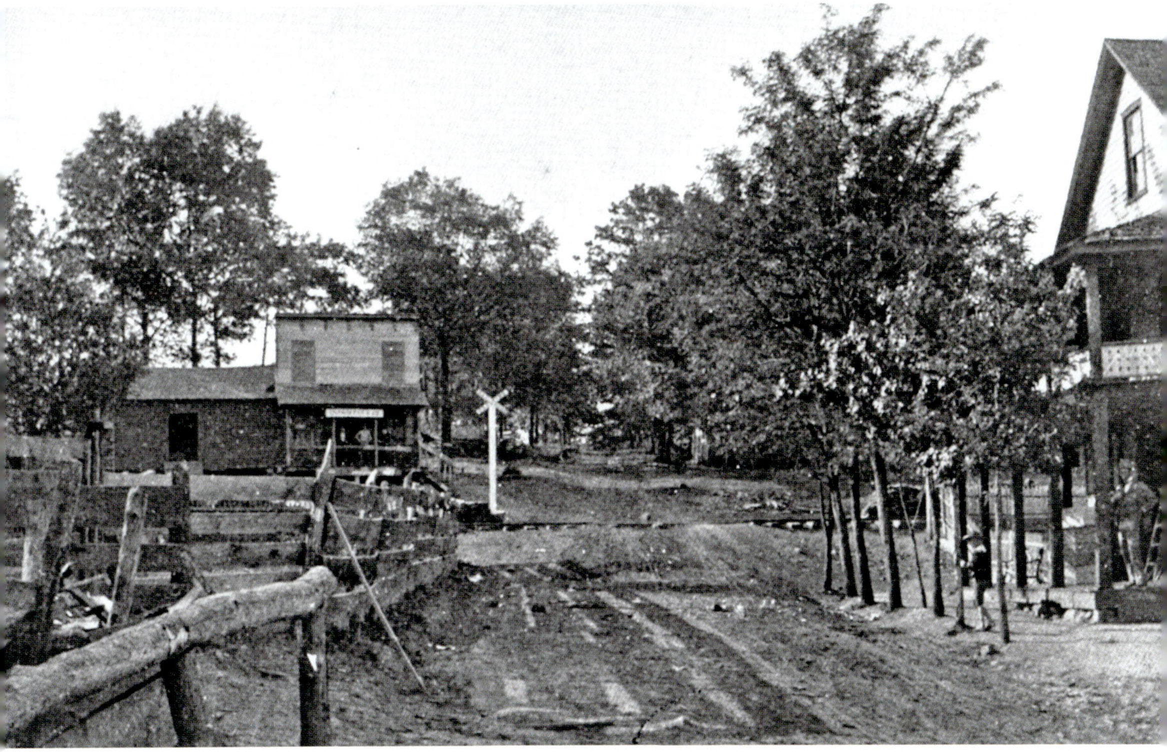

The Silas F. Dougherty house stands on the far right of the c. 1880s Gertrude Sprague photograph above. Prior to the railroad coming into the valley, Dougherty operated one of the first stores in Black Mountain and a post office near the present location of the Monte Vista Hotel. Mail was delivered by stagecoach. When the mail began to come via train, Dougherty moved his home and store to Stepp Street (now Black Mountain Avenue), across the railroad tracks from the depot. North of the tracks is Enthoffer & Co.

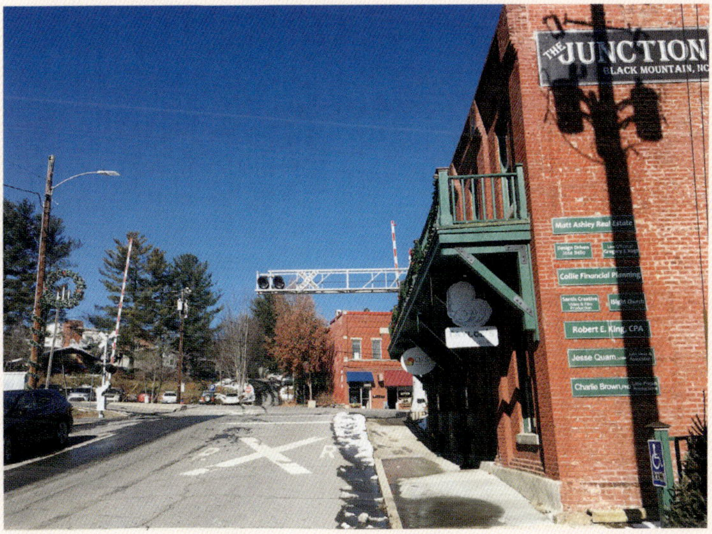

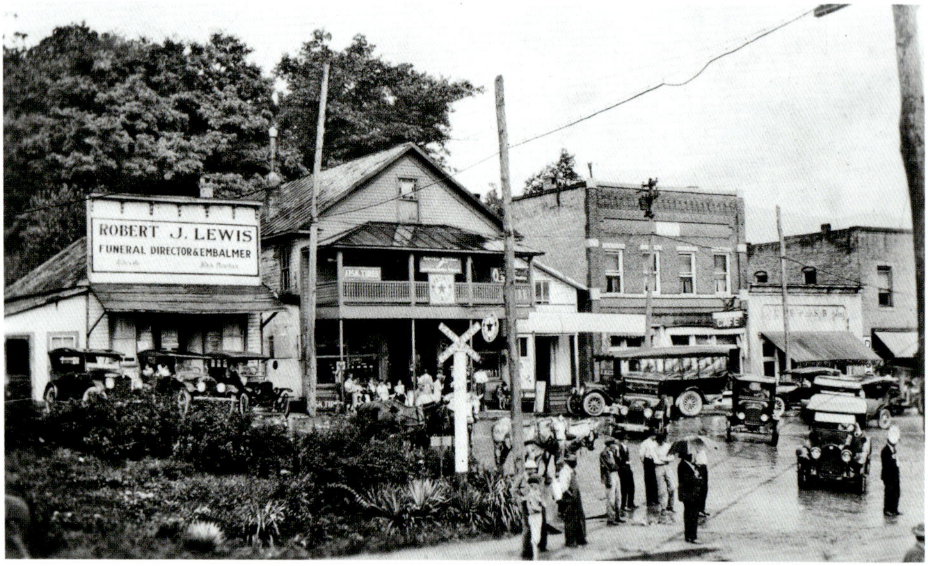

In 1906, Robert J. Lewis came to the area from Pennsylvania "to care for the dead," as he put it. In 1916, Lewis purchased property from the Bradhams northwest of the railroad tracks to operate his eponymous funeral home. Prior to its use as a funeral home, it was Ellis Worth Queen's mercantile store around 1900 and Enthoffer & Co. prior to that. Other buildings in the c. 1920s photograph above include The People's Bank, at right, and the Sam Papas building, the two-story brick building at center. Around this time, the Papas building was home to the New York Café, which at one time was run by John and Claudia McGraw. Today, only the Papas building still stands. It is home to Antiques on Sutton.

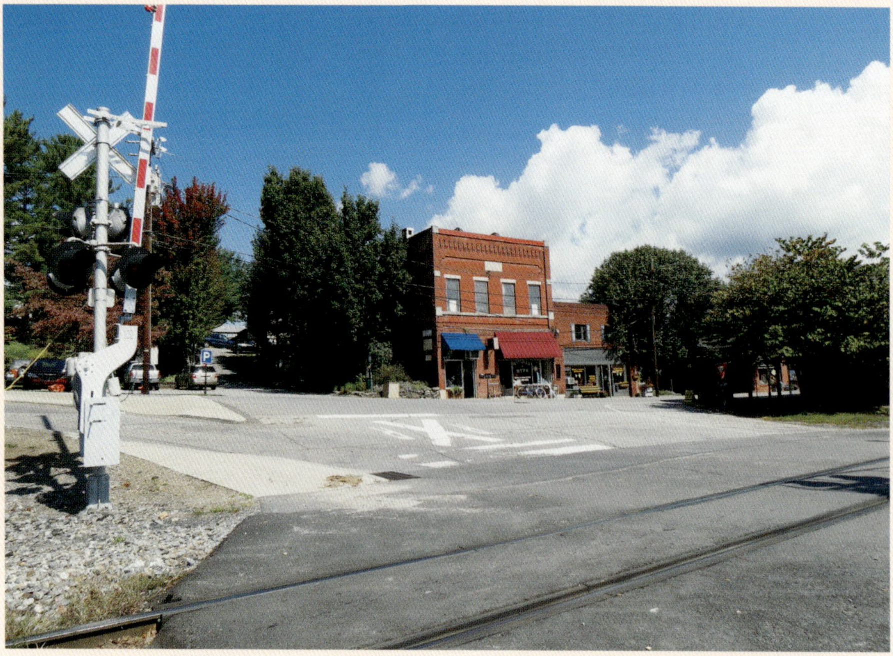

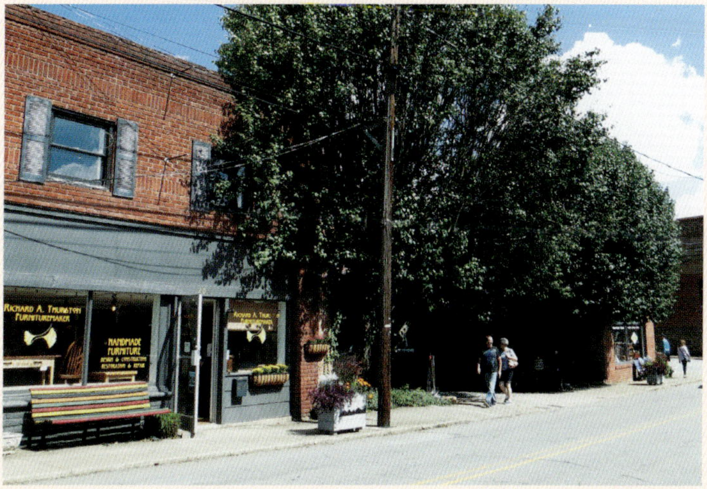

The 1909 photograph below shows Sutton Avenue as it intersects with Cherry Street at the far right. At far left is the Black Mountain Barber Shop, which would later become Black Mountain Pharmacy, and then The People's Bank. The two-story building next door was a drugstore that also sold candy and soda. Dr. Clifford Porter operated his drugstore across from the depot with Elijah Kerlee serving as his assistant. When Porter constructed a new building in 1925 (now part of Town Hardware), the pharmacy and soda fountain were taken over by George Kirpatrick and Lawrence Wheelon. In the mid-1930s, Roy Campbell operated the business for about two years before opening Roy's Inn on old US 70. None of these buildings are still standing.

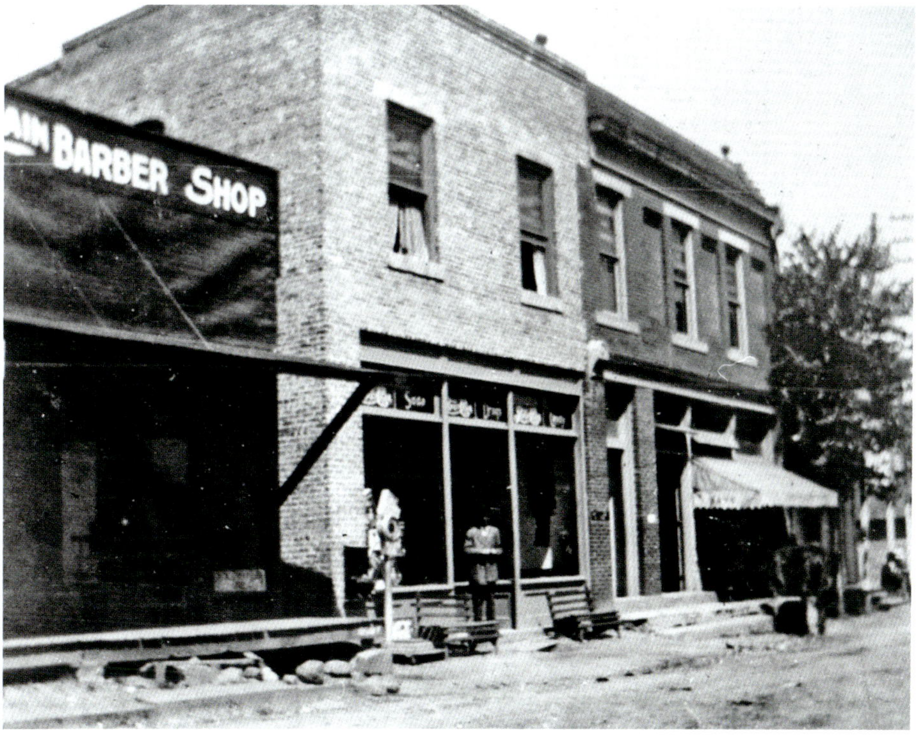

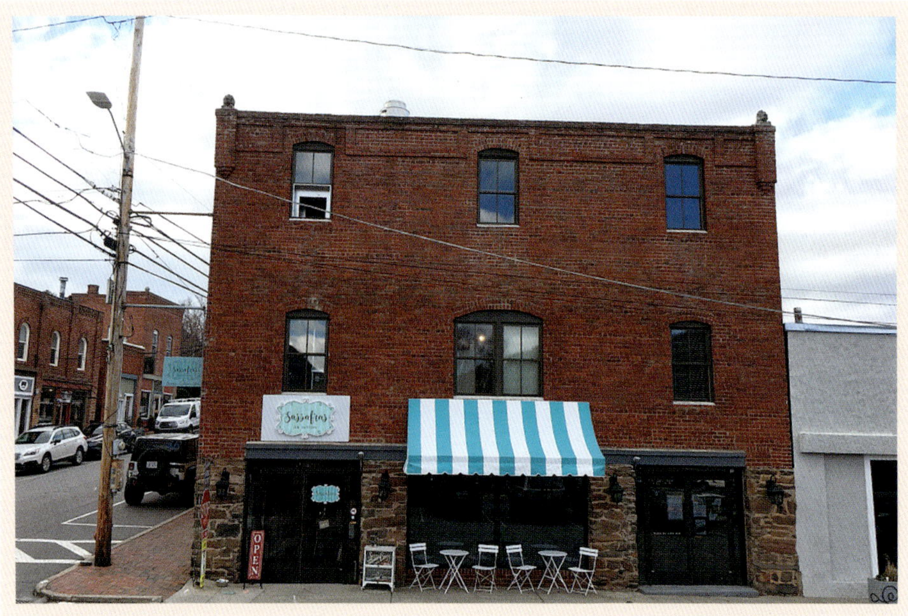

Around 1895, the stone building across from the depot was redeveloped into a livery stable by the Brown brothers, Clarence and Bert. A victim of the 1912 fire, only the stone foundation from the original Brown's livery stable remains. The upper brick portion of the building was built soon after using the same foundation. Following the closure of the livery stable, White-Brown Motor Company—the town's first automobile agency—incorporated in 1923 and operated out of the building. The building is now home to Sassafras on Sutton, a bookstore and coffee shop, and Poppy's Handcrafted Popcorn.

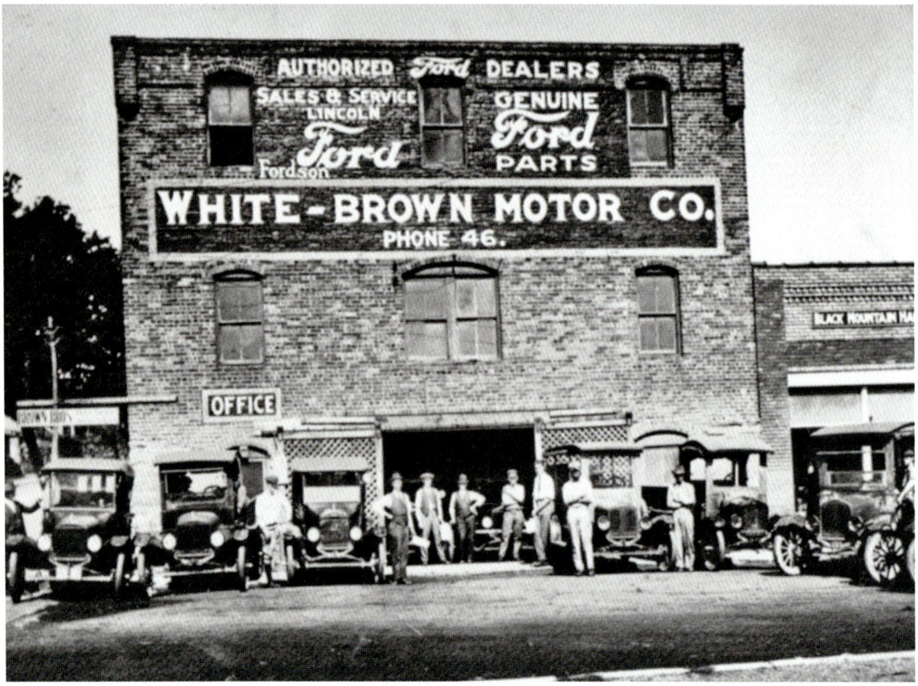

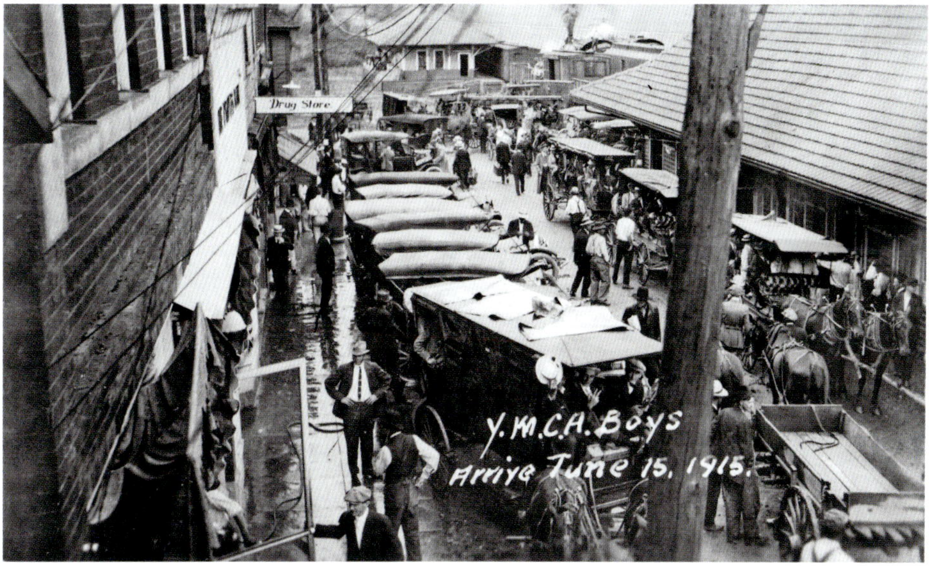

Sutton Avenue is pictured in the June 15, 1915, image above from the Lora Hamby Reed Collection. The depot is at right, and the freight house can be seen in the background. The arriving train unloaded a large group of male students heading to Blue Ridge Assembly to attend the annual YMCA Students' Conference. Though the depot was spared in the 1912 fire, the Southern Railway freight house and its contents were destroyed, an estimated loss of $1,000. It was soon rebuilt and stood until sometime before 1978, when Broadway Avenue was extended across the railroad tracks to connect Black Mountain to the new I-40 interchange.

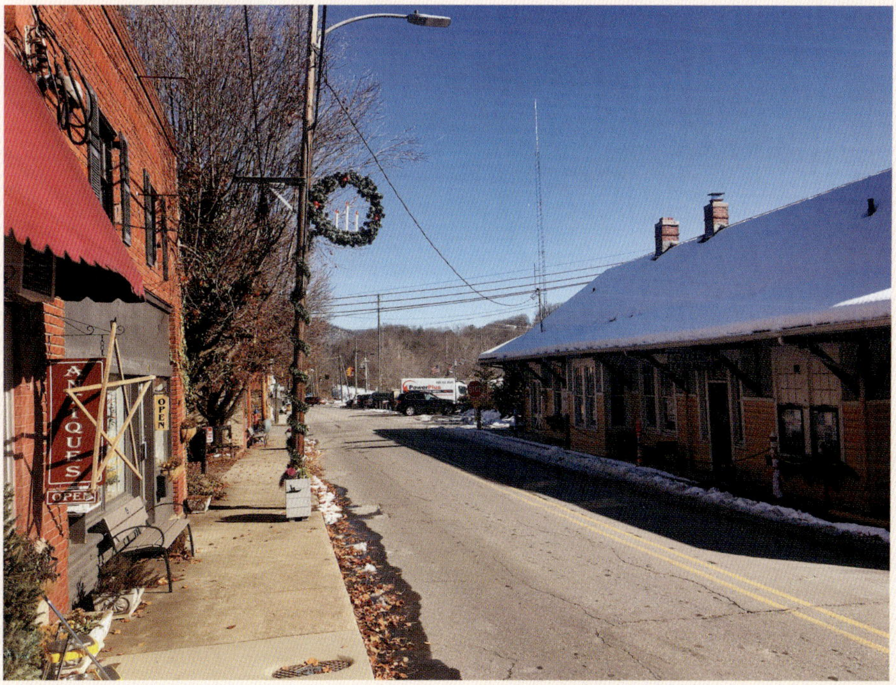

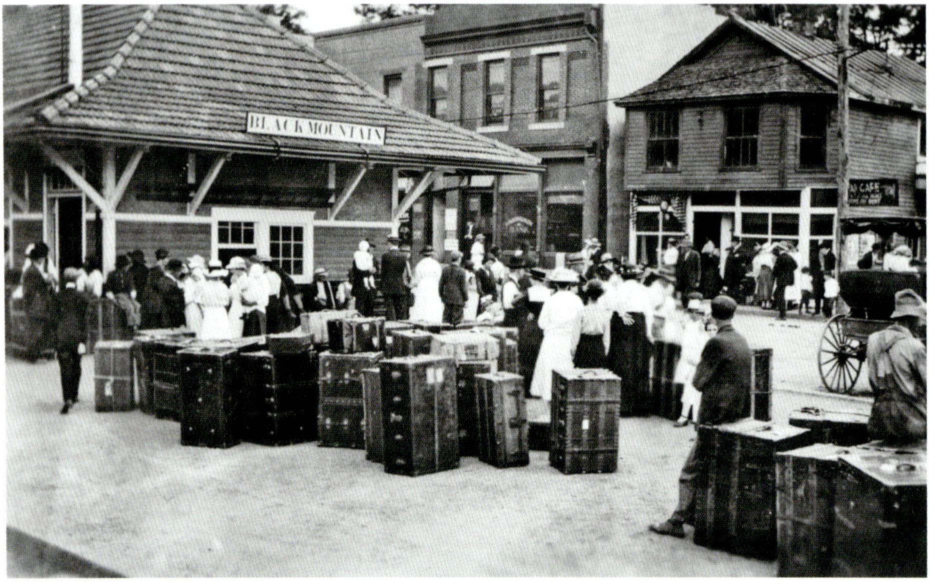

The Commonwealth Bank and the Star Café on Sutton Avenue are in the background of the c. 1917 photograph above from the Lora Hamby Reed Collection. The Commonwealth Bank began doing business in 1907 but failed in 1931, a consequence of the Depression. Though it did not burn during the 1912 fire, a brick was thrown through the plate glass window in a suspected attempt at robbery. Upstairs was D. Eckles Law Firm. Next door, in the present-day location of Chifferobe Home and Garden, was the Star Café, which was in operation during the mid- to late 1910s. The sign in front of the café reads, "Locks on All Doors, Rooms for Rent." The building was demolished after the 1920s, and the current building was constructed in 1946 by Finley Stepp as Stepp's restaurant.

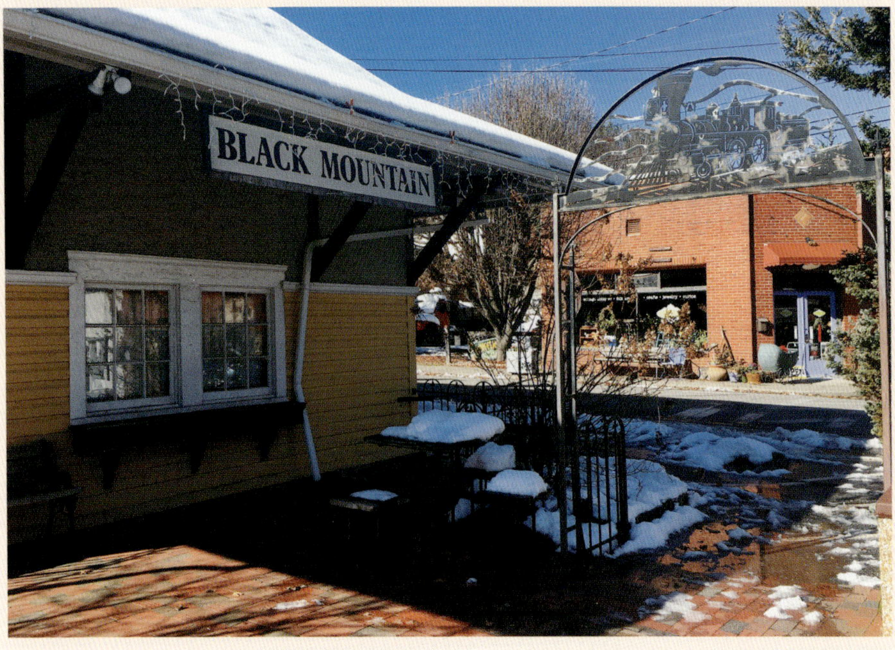

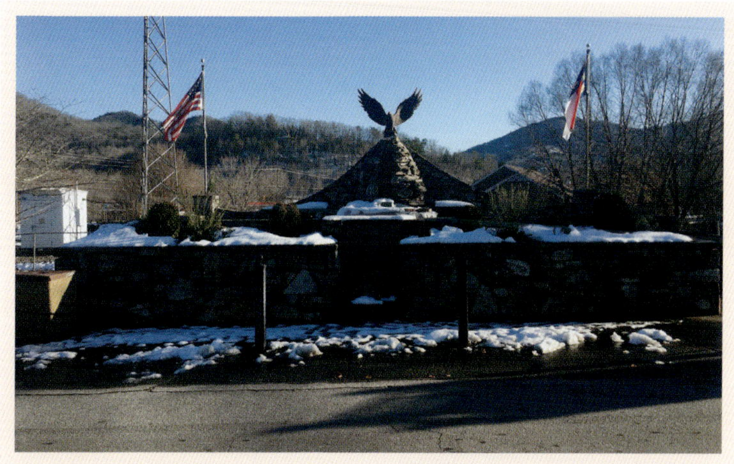

John Mitchell Melton (1869–1952) operated Melton's Meat Market in the early 20th century. The photograph below, believed to have been taken around 1910 on Sutton Avenue, shows John (right) and his son Harvey Dula Melton (1897–1959). In the 1920s, the Melton family had a meat market on Cherry Street. Harvey married Rona Victoria Anderson (1902–1920) in 1919, and the following year, they had a son, Harvey Dula Jr. Both John and Harvey Sr. worked as butchers for their entire careers. Though the specific location of the meat market is unknown, it may have been near the Grey Eagle monument on Sutton Avenue.

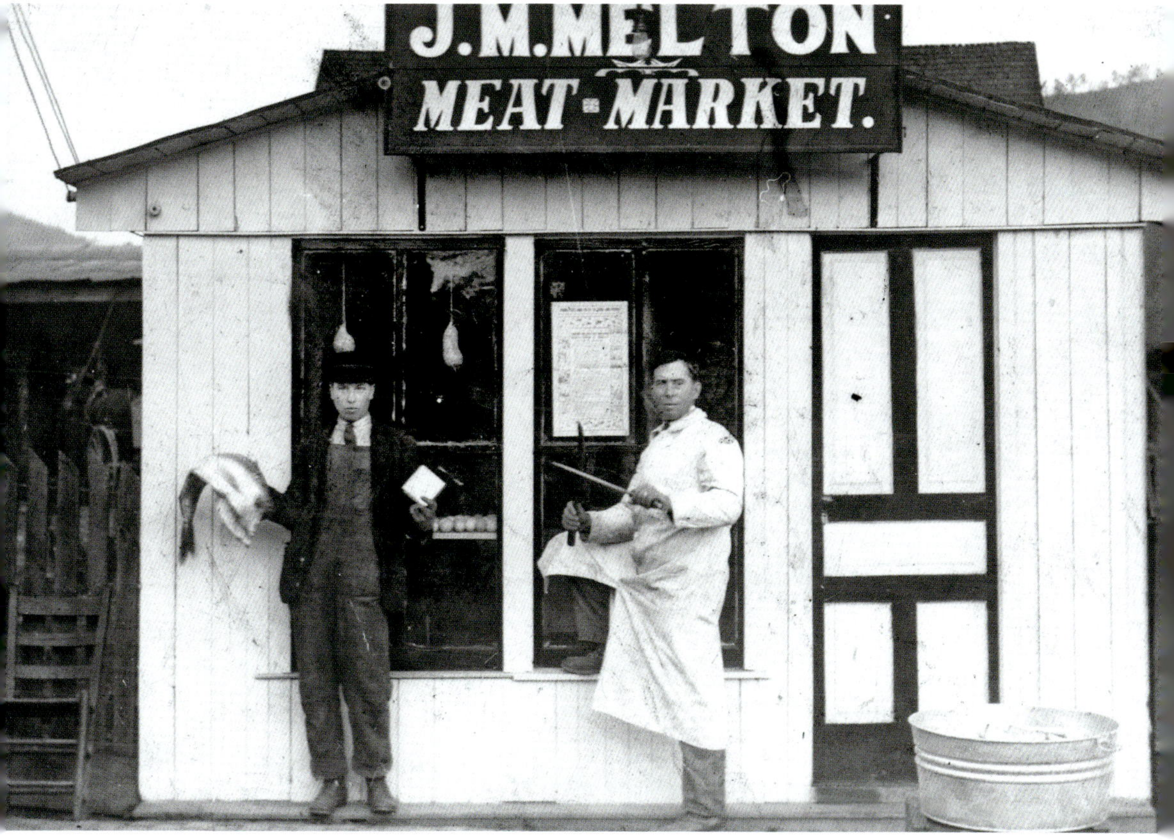

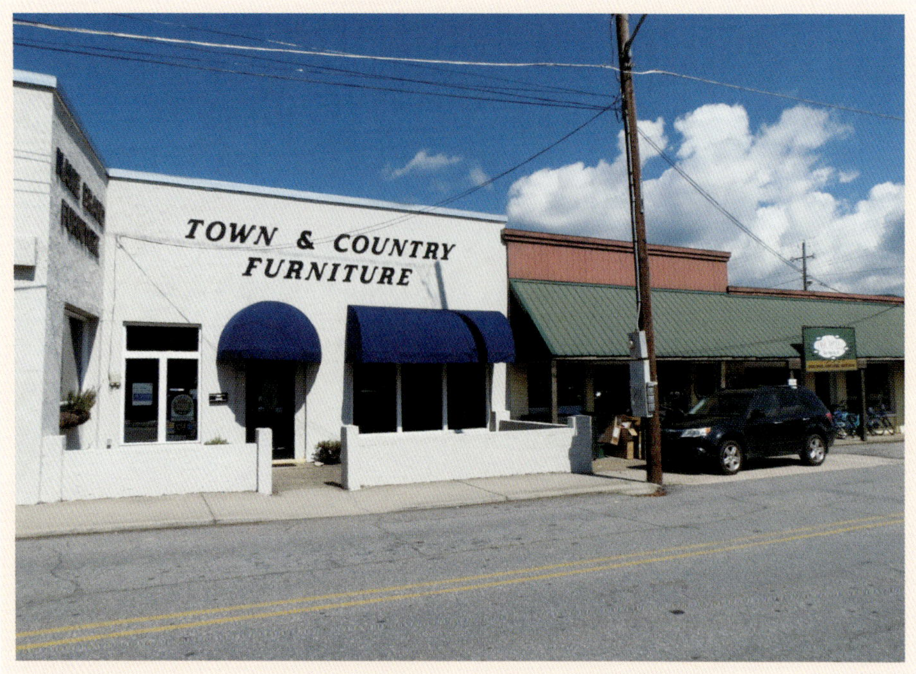

The c. 1923 photograph of Black Mountain Lumber Company below shows, from left to right, Floyd Dennis, Susan Hooker, Ike Cook, Connely Dougherty, Alf Tyson, Merida Hodgins, John Burgess, and R. Long. Land deeds indicate that Black Mountain Lumber Company was chartered and built in 1908. Sometime around 1914, the company was transferred to Walter, Connely, and L.L. Dougherty and Floyd Dennis. According to Joyce Justus Parris in *A History of Black Mountain*, Walter died young, and Connely's son James managed the company with Floyd. Though the facade has changed dramatically since 1923, the original building still stands and is part of Epic Cycles on Sutton Avenue.

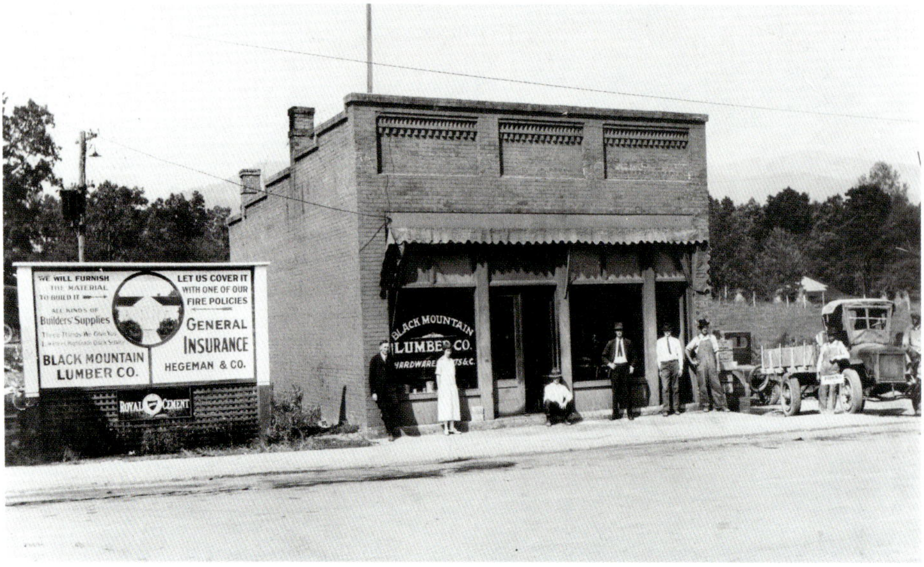

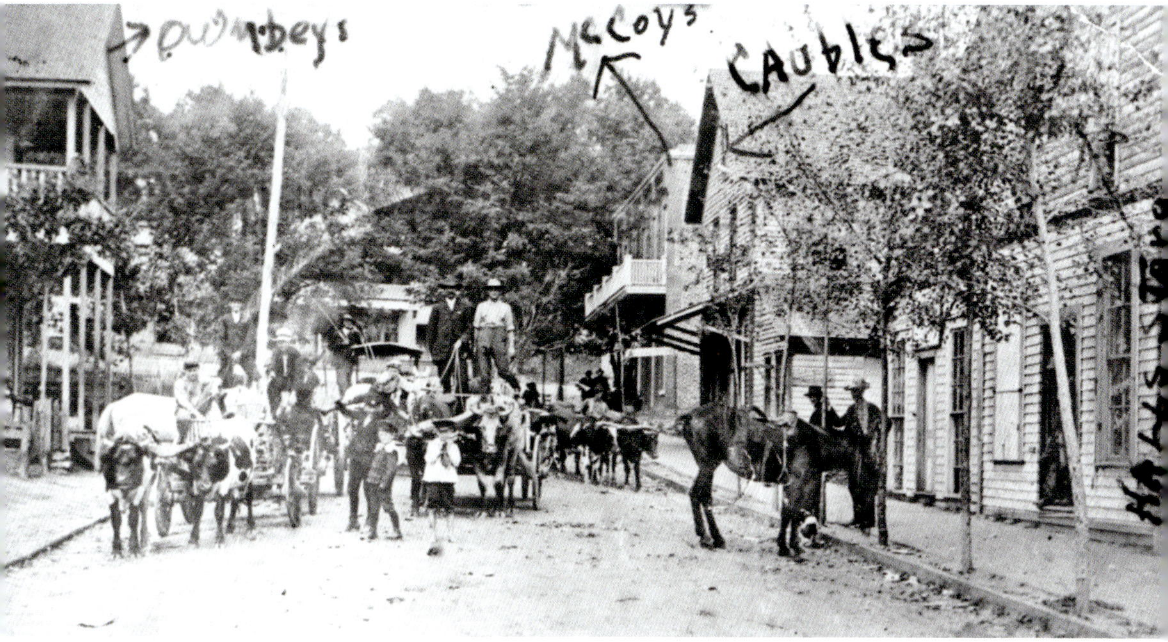

Now known as Black Mountain Avenue, South Main Street (also often referred to as Stepp Street) runs south perpendicular to the railroad tracks directly west of the depot. The only building still standing from the 1912 photograph above is the McKoy building, the two-story brick building in the back right corner. Hall's Store was a large general store run by the Hall family. The building labeled "Caubles" is the Silas F. Dougherty home and store, seen on page 13.

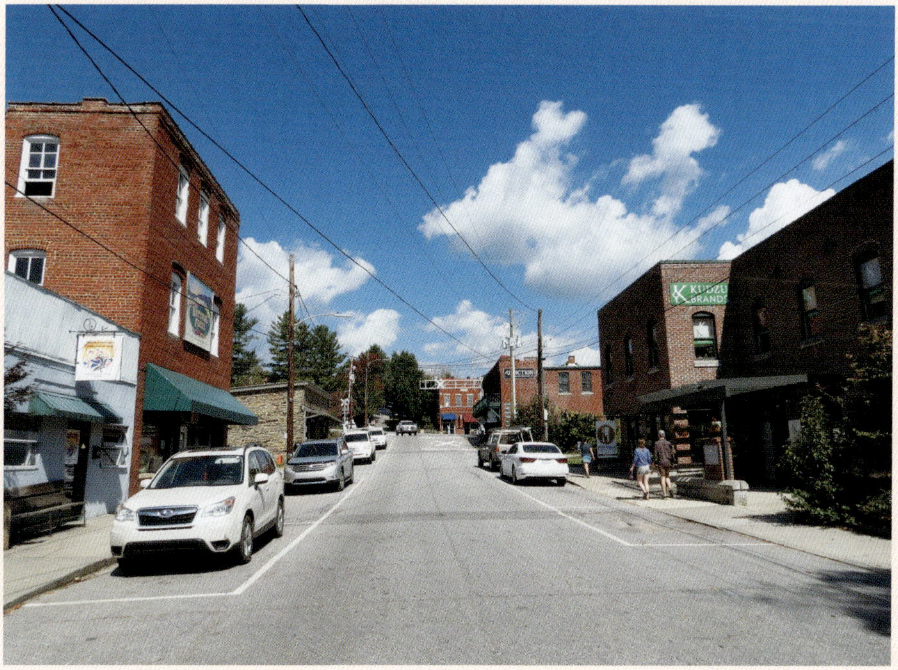

One of the oldest buildings still standing in Black Mountain's historic downtown was built around 1890 by J.W. McKoy as a grocery store. McKoy served as president of Commonwealth Bank in 1907 and as Black Mountain's mayor from 1913 to 1914. The building replaced an earlier wooden store owned by his father. In 1905, Black Mountain rented the building's basement as the first town hall. In 1918, the building was used as a hospital to care for the large number of people affected by the influenza pandemic. By the 1930s, it housed Hipp's dry goods store, followed by storage for the nearby Black Mountain Hosiery Mill. The second floor was a boardinghouse. The building is now home to Que Sera restaurant on the ground floor and several small businesses on the second floor.

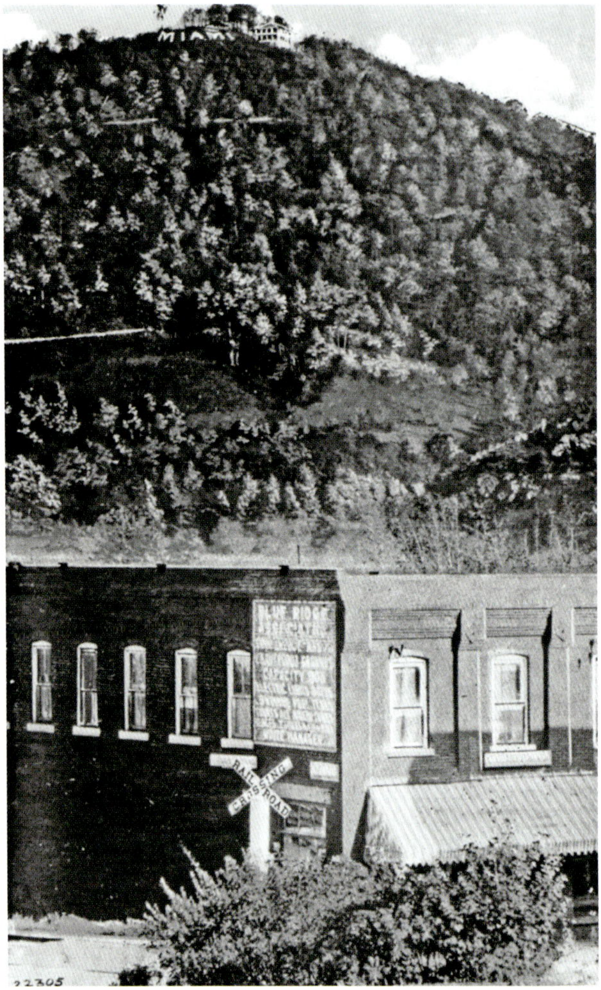

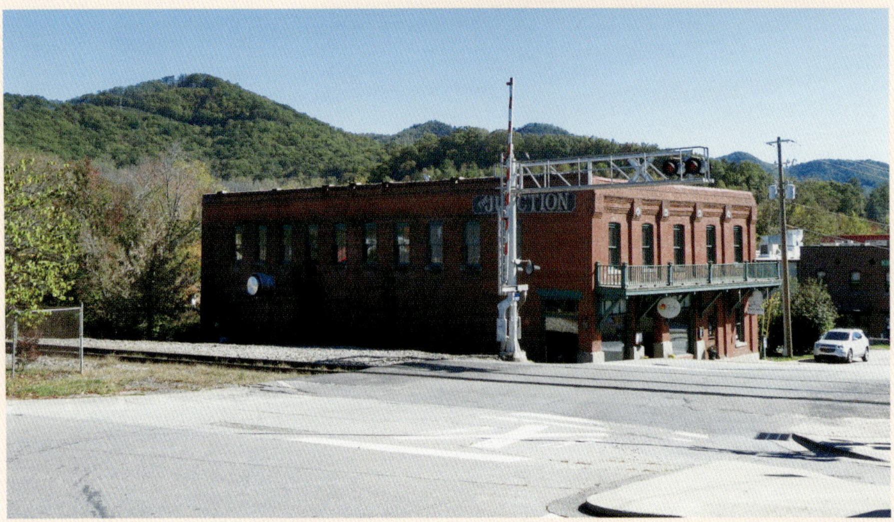

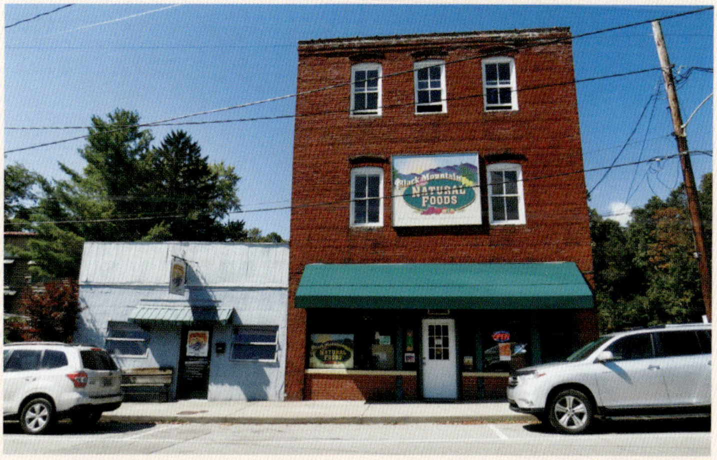

On the far left of the photograph of Black Mountain High School's 1916 graduating class below is John Edward Whitaker. The Evans Building, in the background, housed one of the town's early post offices. The building was constructed on Black Mountain Avenue in 1908 for William C. Hall (1855–1919), the town's postmaster from 1913 until he passed away. The post office later moved to one of the buildings now owned by Tyson Furniture on Broadway Avenue, before it relocated to its present location on Richardson Boulevard in the 1960s. The Evans Building was named for Hall's daughter Willa Hall Evans (1884–1959), who operated a boardinghouse on its second and third floors. Besides the post office, Hall and then his daughter operated a dry goods store on the lower level until 1955. The building later became Williams Brothers Oil Company and is now home to Black Mountain Natural Foods. (Then, courtesy of Ann Whitaker McAllister Collection.)

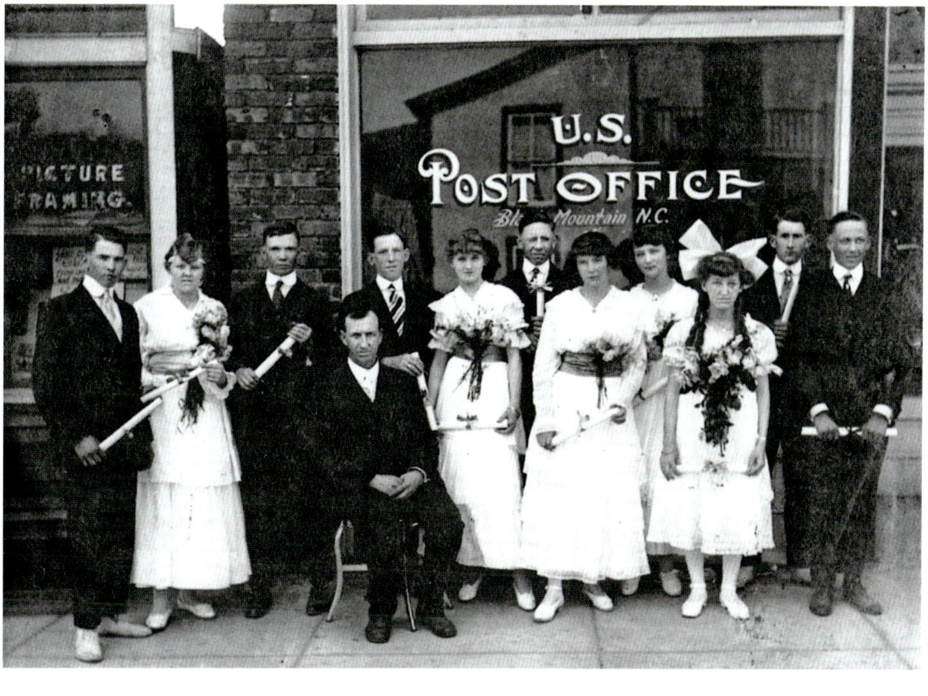

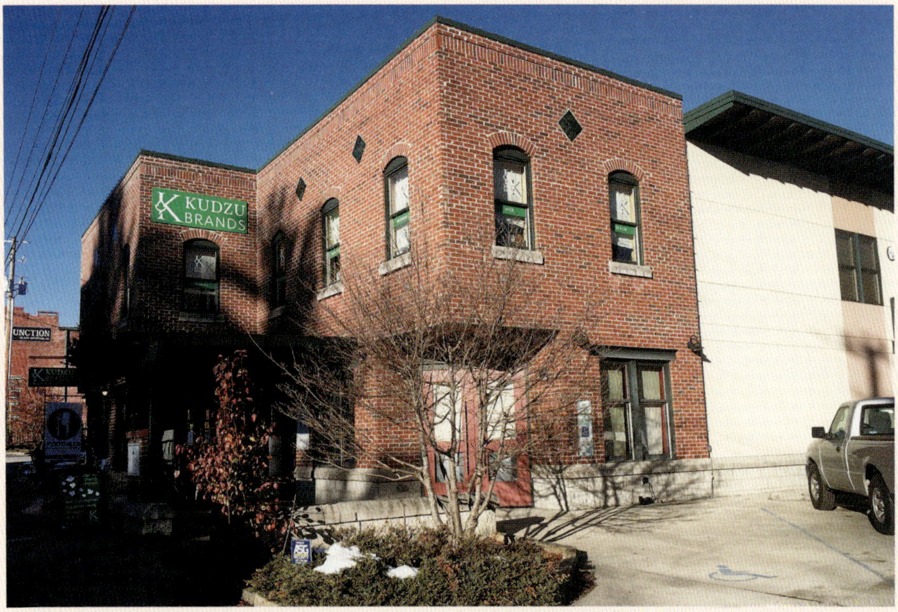

Dr. Arthur McKee Dula came to Black Mountain from Old Fort and built the home and store in the c. 1900s photograph below. It stood in the approximate location of Kudzu Brands, as can be seen in the aerial view on page 11. Dula married Cora Stepp, the daughter of George W. Stepp, who erected the home that is now Louise's Kitchen on the corner of Vance and Black Mountain Avenues around 1907. Stepp was employed as a cabinetmaker and also worked on the Biltmore Estate before serving as Black Mountain's mayor from 1908 to 1911 and 1915 to 1917.

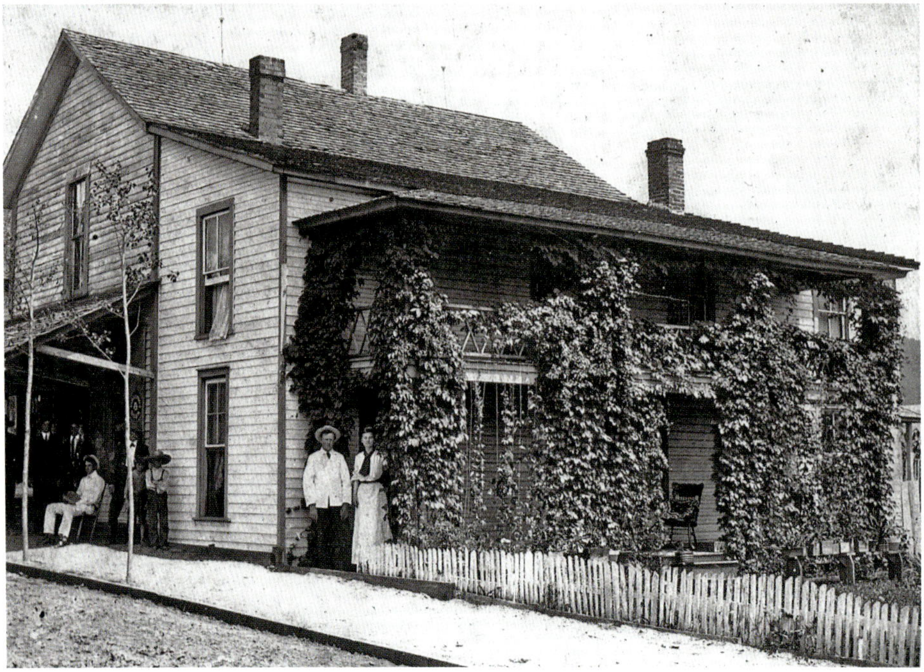

CHAPTER 2

After the Fire

Cherry Street and Broadway Avenue

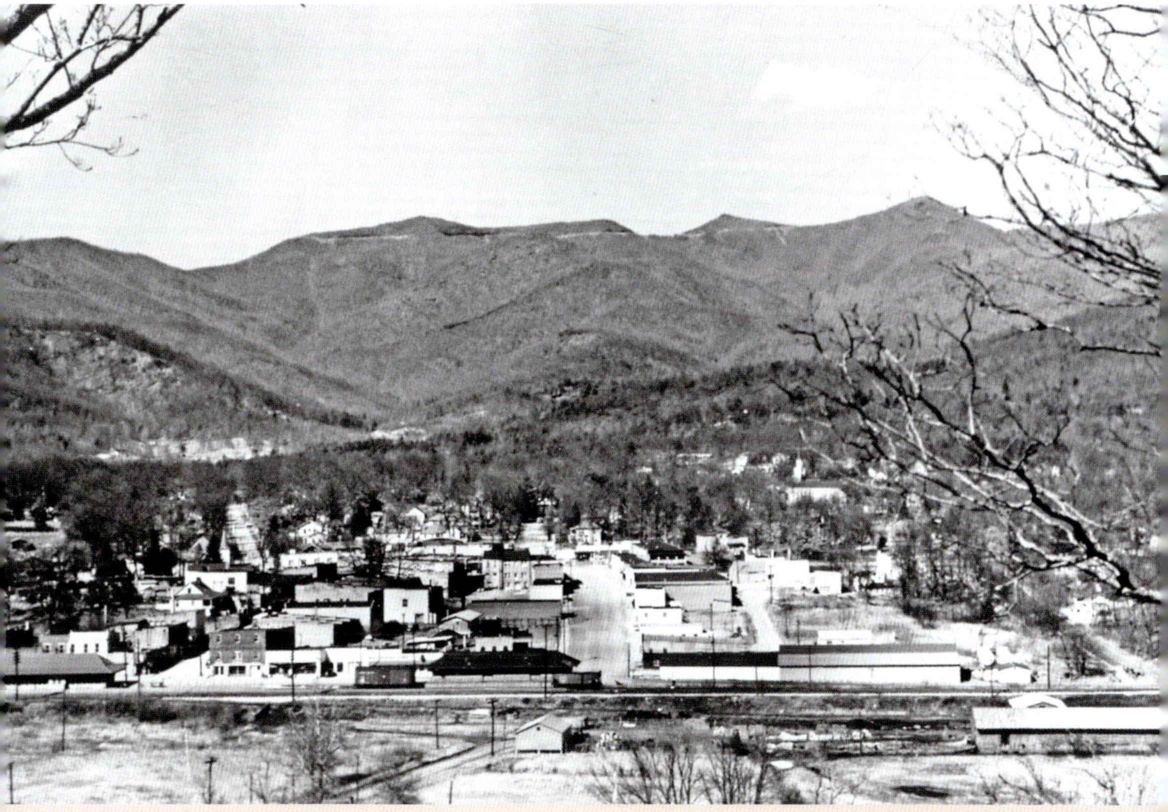

Most of the buildings on Cherry Street and Broadway Avenue were constructed after the fire of 1912. Here, Broadway Avenue only runs from its intersection with State Street in the north to its intersection with Sutton Avenue and the railroad tracks in the south. However, when Interstate 40 was constructed, a railroad crossing was built to connect Broadway Avenue to the interstate on-ramps on North Carolina Route 9. In 1975, the town asked the state highway administration to provide an overpass from Route 9 over the tracks to Broadway Avenue, but the state rejected the proposal in favor of the current grade crossing due to limited funding and time.

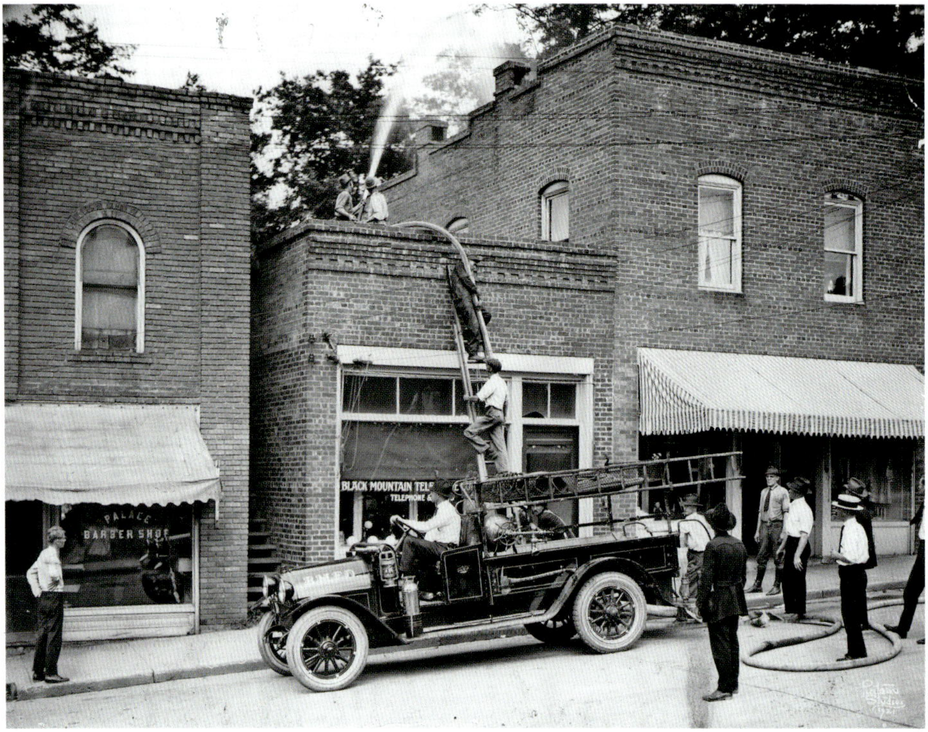

Above, the Black Mountain Fire Department fights a fire in 1921 from the roof of the buildings that now house Dark City Deli in this Plateau Studios photograph. At that time, the Black Mountain Telephone Corporation (1907–1925) operated in the middle building (built in 1916), the Palace Barber Shop in the lower building (built in 1914), and Jones Spence Wahab's dry goods store in the upper building (built in 1914), likely a replacement after Wahab lost his store in the 1912 fire. This building would become part of Weldon Early's dry-cleaning service after 1934 along with the upper building. The Palace Barber Shop building was constructed as a feed and seed store. J.W. Kincaid operated the barber shop through the 1920s, 1930s, and 1940s. It was advertised as being "free from intoxicating drinks."

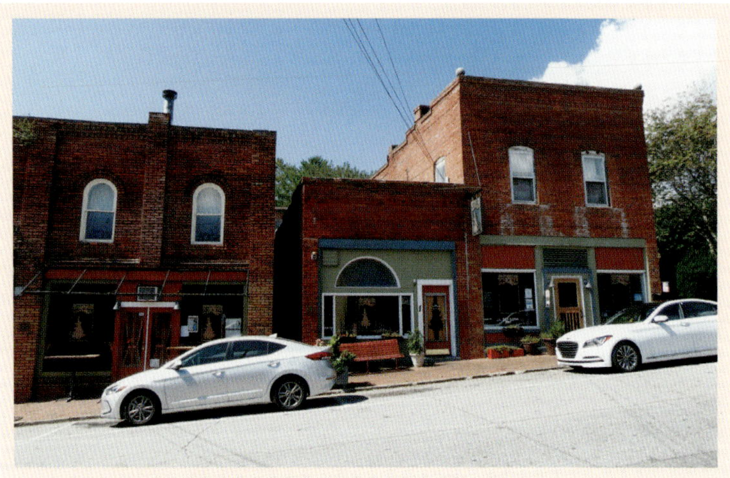

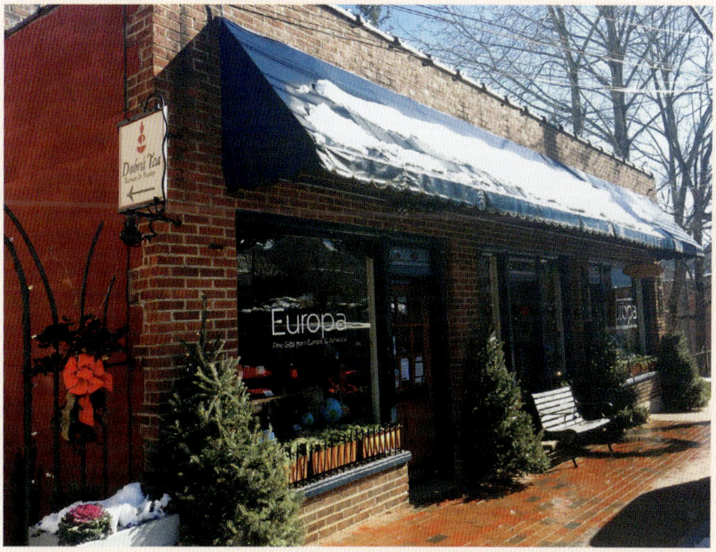

On southeast Cherry Street, J. Guy Green, pictured below, ran Hol'n One Donuts from the 1950s to the 1980s in the northern storefront, where he also sold hamburgers. Married to Nell Grist Green, he had one son, Ronald. According to Black Mountain's listing in the National Register of Historic Places, Ronald operated the Western Union telegraph office until the late 1950s. Guy bought the one-story brick building, constructed in 1939, from Harry and Hassie Pearl Wade in 1950. In 1972, he transferred the building to Ronald, who used the southern storefront as Ronald Green Business Service, an accounting firm. It is now home to Europa.

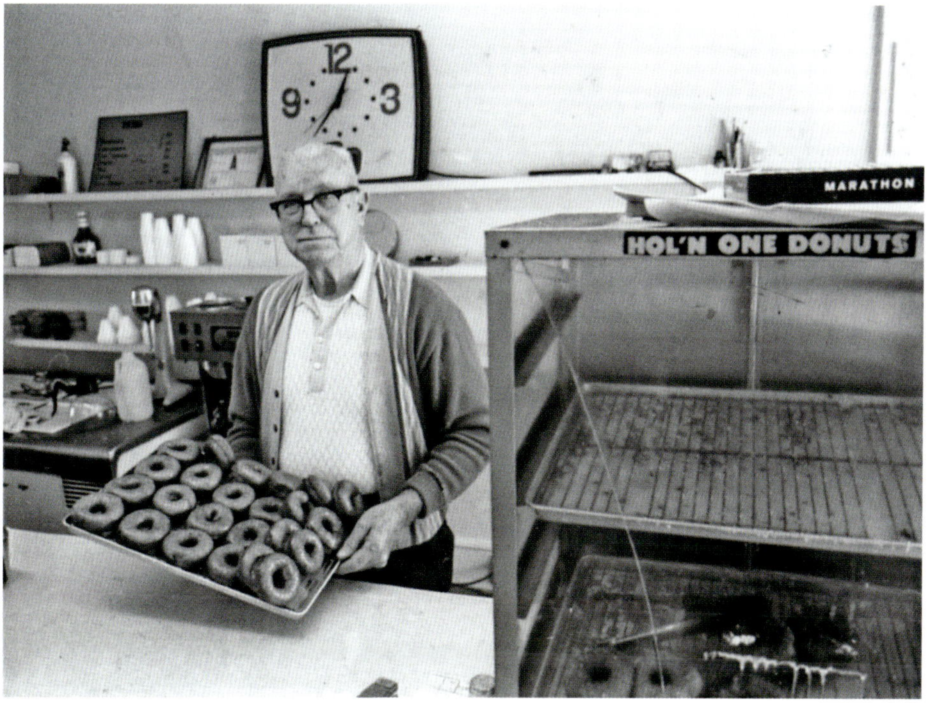

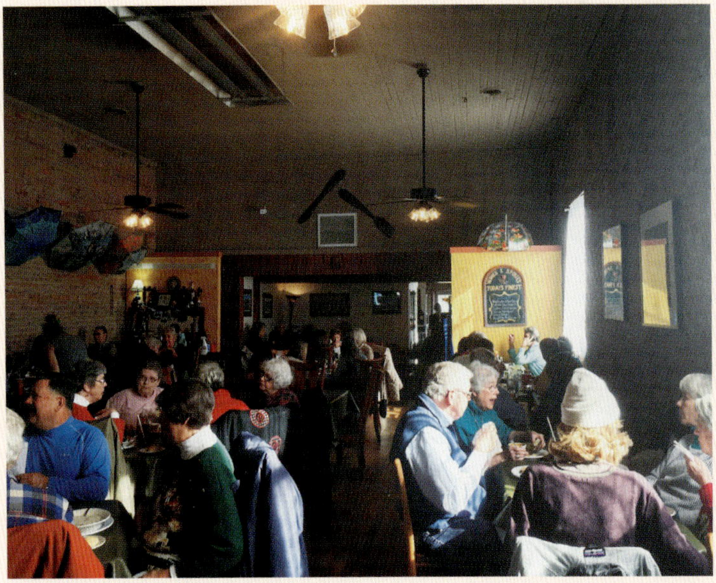

Lonnie Washington Morgan managed the Morgan, Kinsey & Company Store on Cherry Street, formerly Briggs Street, during the 1910s. The store sold general merchandise, dry goods, groceries, and shoes. In the c. 1914 photograph below, five of his six children pose with him inside the store. Though raised in nearby Fairview, Morgan made his career in Black Mountain. He taught in the county schools, served as mayor from 1911 to 1913, and was police chief. He also ran for Buncombe County sheriff. Morgan drowned in 1919 when his car veered into Flat Creek while he was delivering mail from Black Mountain to Blue Ridge. The building is currently home to Veranda Café.

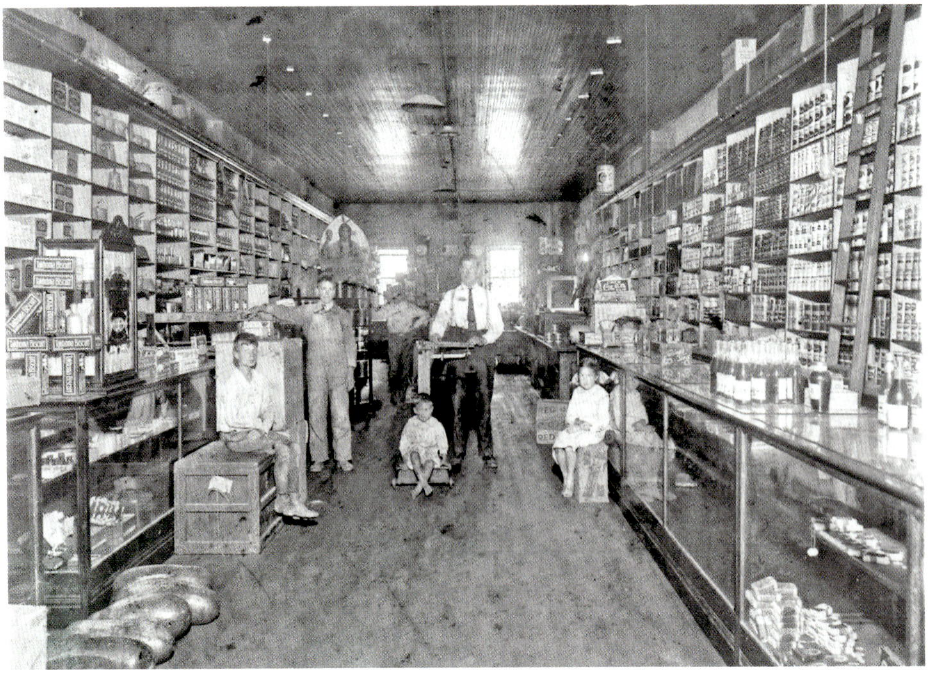

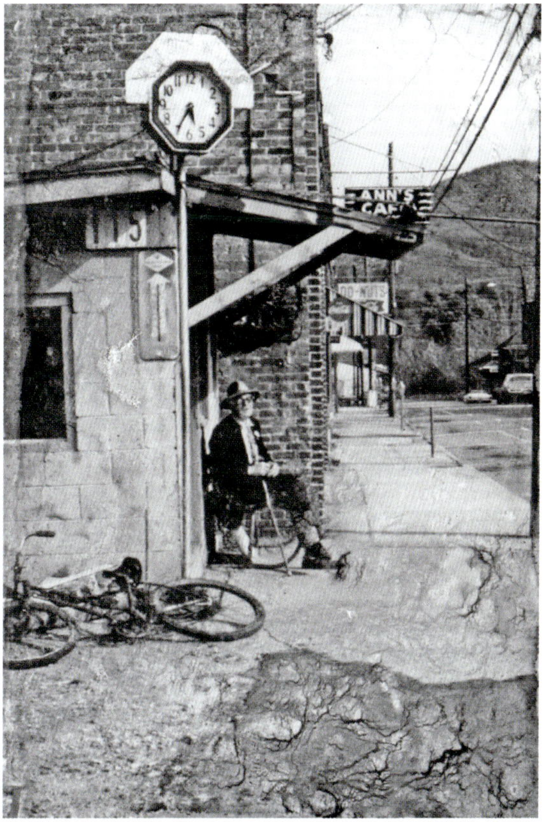

The c. 1965 photograph at left looks south down Cherry Street. At 115 Cherry Street was Blue Diamond Cab Company, operated in Black Mountain and Swannanoa by Clarence Everett Howell. When Howell died in 1982 at 66 years old, he had owned the company for 35 years. It had also been known as the Swannanoa Valley Cab Company. South of the cab stand was Ann's Café, which was operated by Ann Hodson from about 1940 until 1982, when David Peele purchased the building as a new location for McDibb's, now Veranda Café. The cab company's location is now home to Black Mountain's public restrooms.

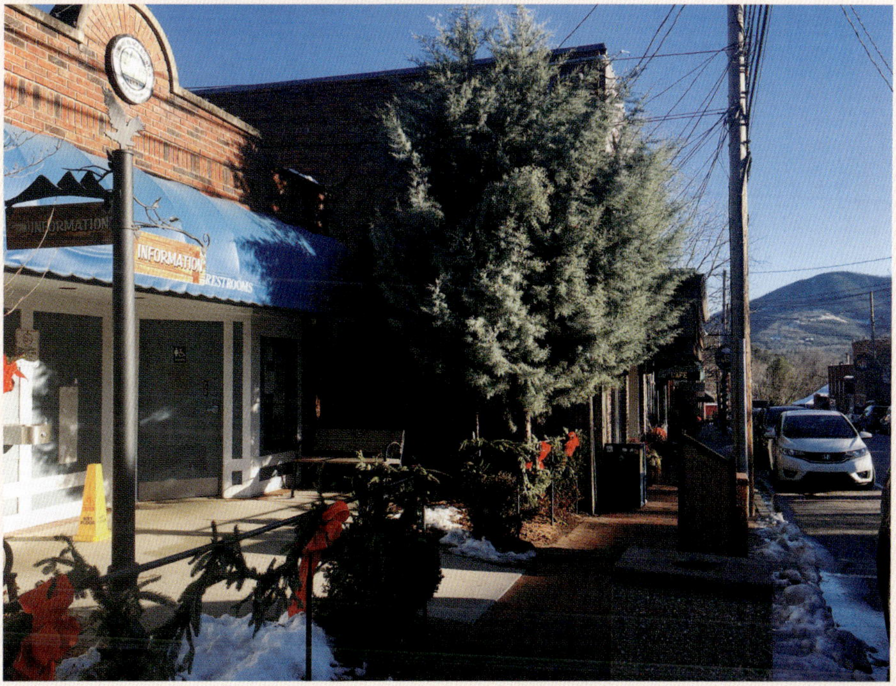

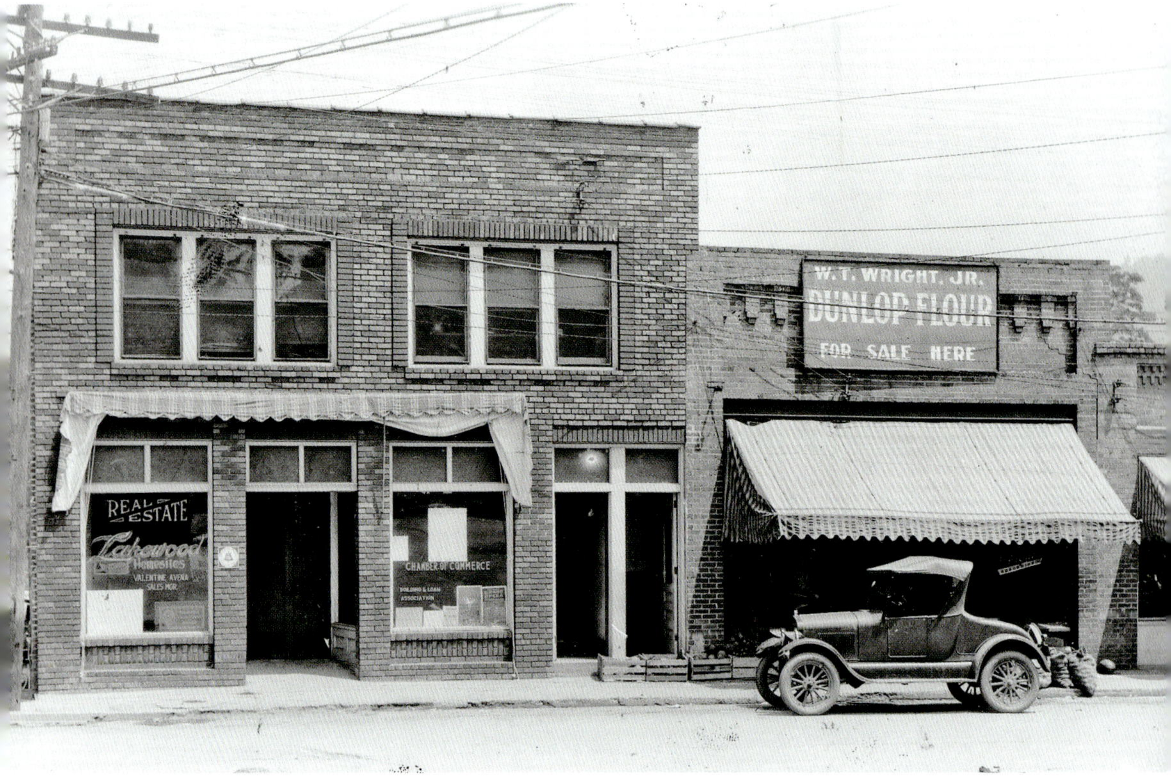

Built around 1920, the building at left, which is now home to Cherry Street Kids, was originally Winfred Hall's clothing store. In the mid-1930s, Frank Groves operated his shoe store out of the building. In the 1924 photograph above, the north side of the building is home to Valentine Avena's real estate office, and the south side of the building contains the town's chamber of commerce offices. The building at right was constructed around 1920 for Wright's Groceries. W.T. Wright Jr. moved his store to State Street in the early 1930s. The building was then occupied by W.T.'s brother Jasper N. Wright's grocery, followed by Marcellous Melton's meat market. It is now home to Black Mountain Books.

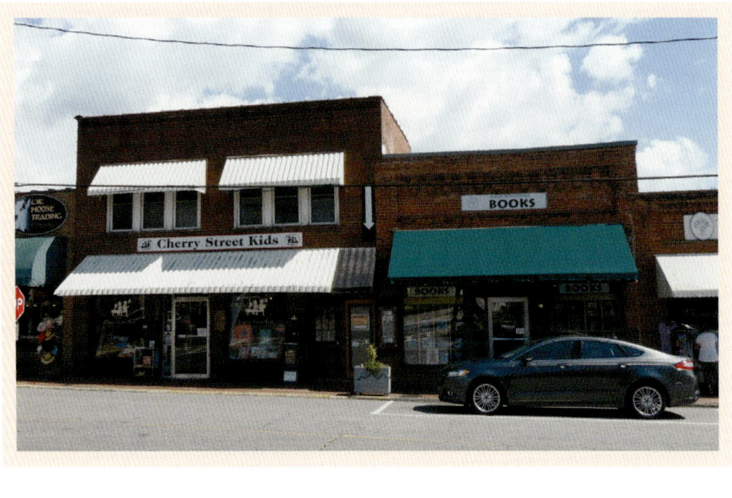

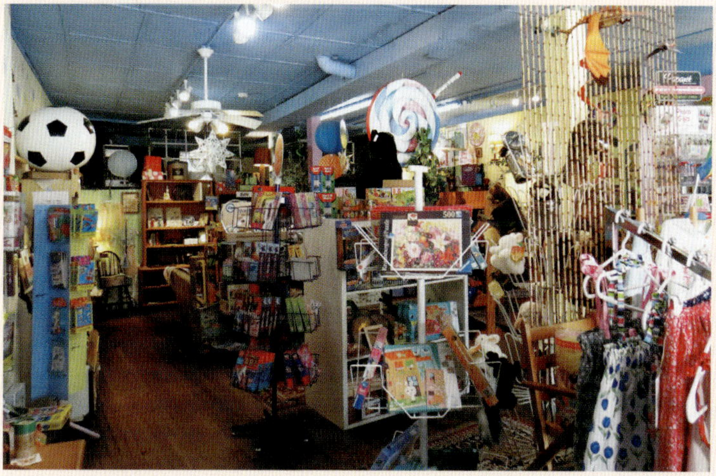

Bertha Jones (at right below) ran a grocery store with her husband, Douglas, in the building that is now Cherry Street Kids. Douglas had been the meat man at the local A&P but left to start the independent Jones Food Store in 1947. After Douglas's death in 1968, Bertha continued running the store. When it opened, it was one of eight groceries in the downtown area. When Bertha closed the store in 1972 due to declining health, it was the only store that remained. She lived in the apartment on the second floor until moving to Highland Farms in 1988. Bertha died in 1995 at the age of 95.

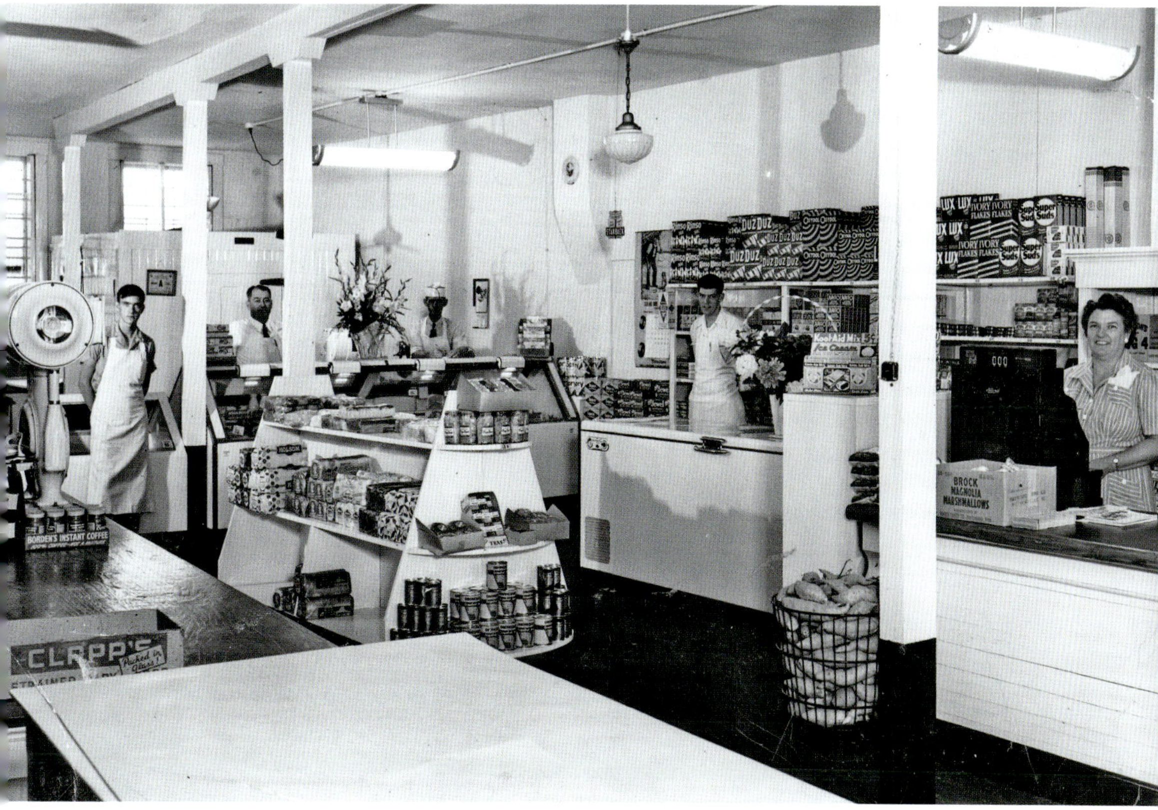

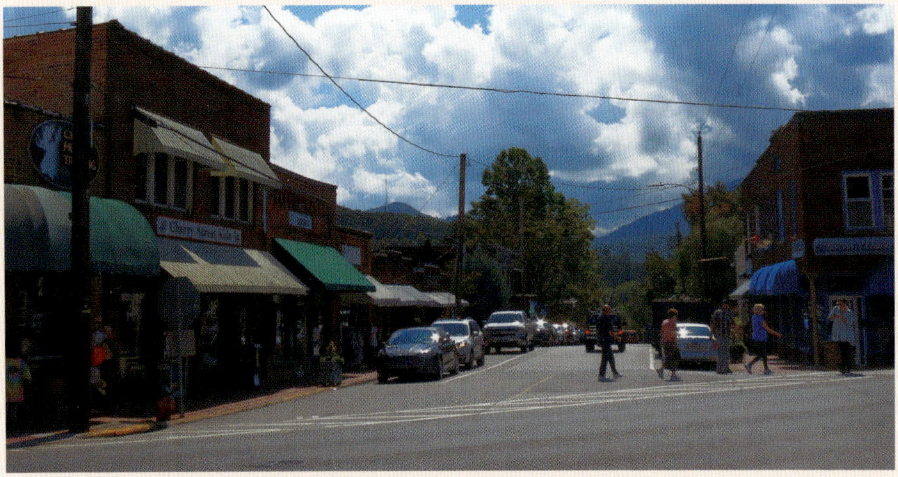

The 1924 photograph below was taken from State Street looking south down Cherry Street. On the right, on the second floor of the building, are the offices of Mount Mitchell Motor Road. On the ground floor, in the present location of Visions of Creation, is H&W Real Estate. The Mount Mitchell Motor Road opened in 1922, allowing travelers to drive (for a small toll) from Black Mountain to Camp Alice near the highest peak in eastern North America, Mount Mitchell. The officers of the company, who likely worked from the offices on the corner of Cherry Street, were Fred A. Perley, president and treasurer; Robert E. Currier, vice president; R.R. Dickey, secretary; and Sandford H. Cohn, promotion and traffic manager.

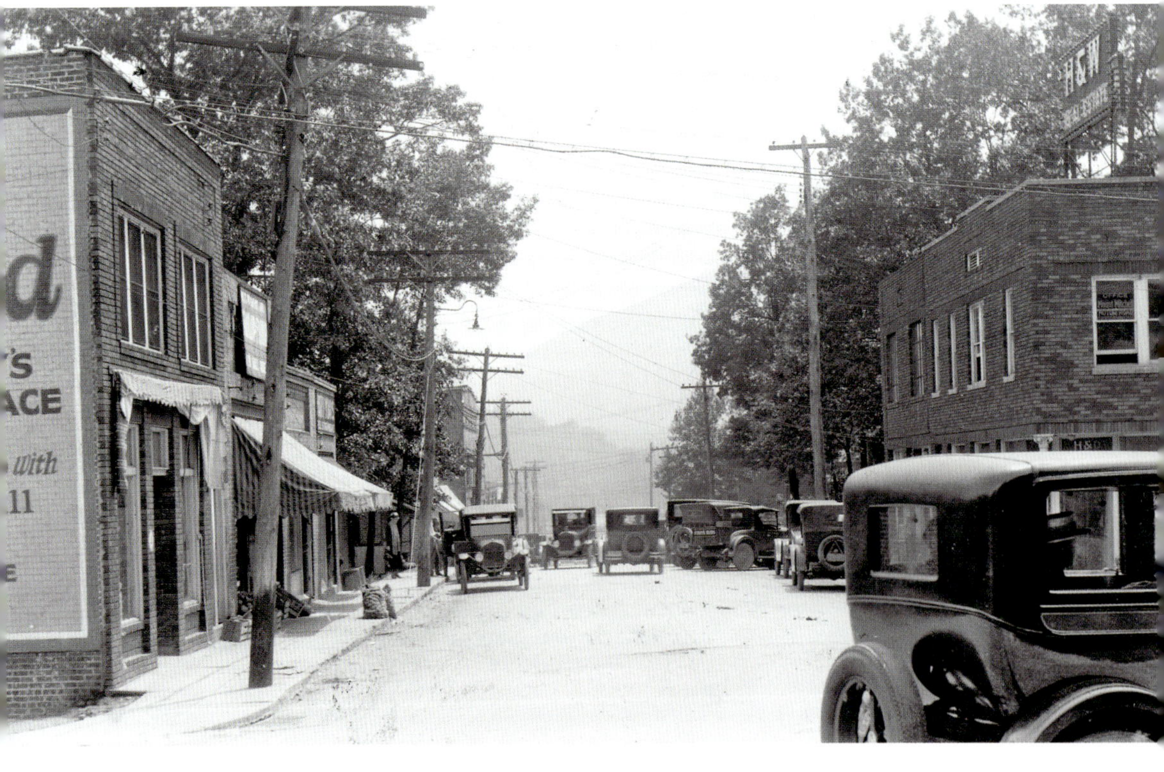

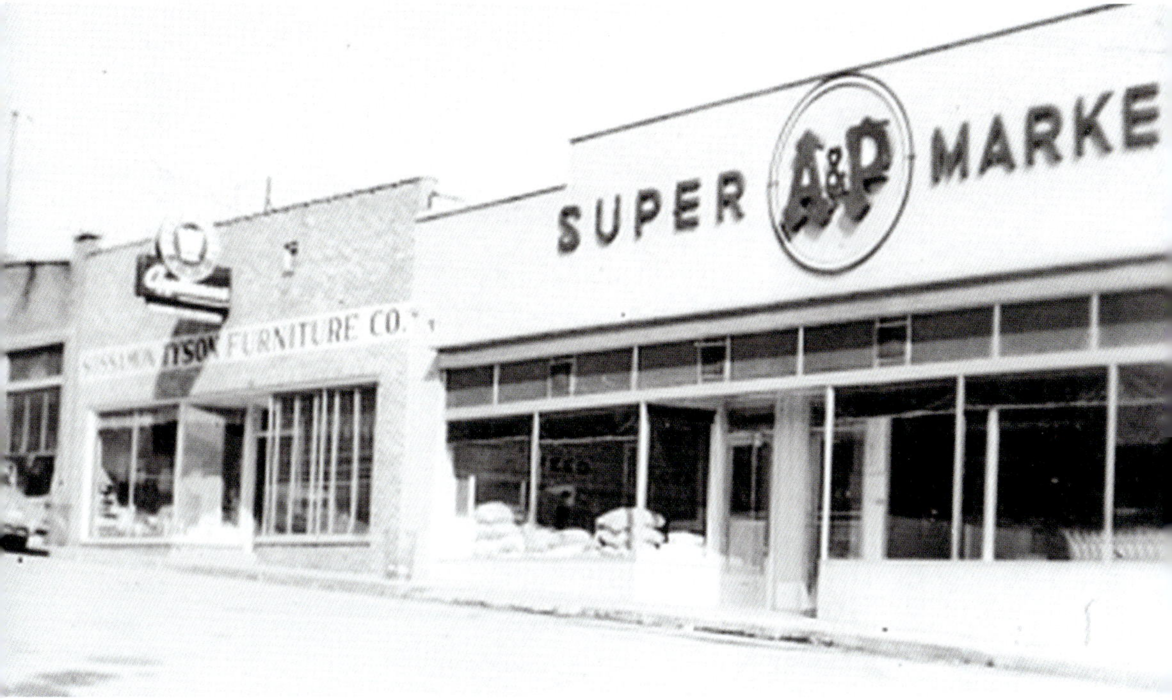

Alfred F. Tyson Jr. built the first showroom for the Sossamon-Tyson Furniture Company in 1946. George Rankin constructed the A&P building to serve the grocery in 1950. The building north of Tyson Furniture was erected by F.B. Dennis in 1927 and served as the Western Union office in the late 1940s. The post office was located in the Dennis building (note the flagpole on top) until 1960, when it moved to its present location on Richardson Boulevard. Now all three buildings are home to Tyson Furniture showrooms.

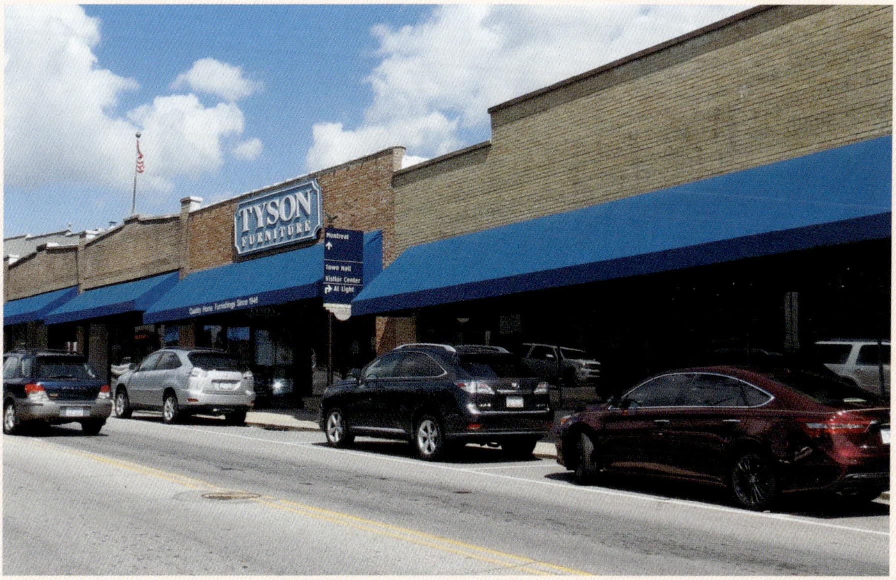

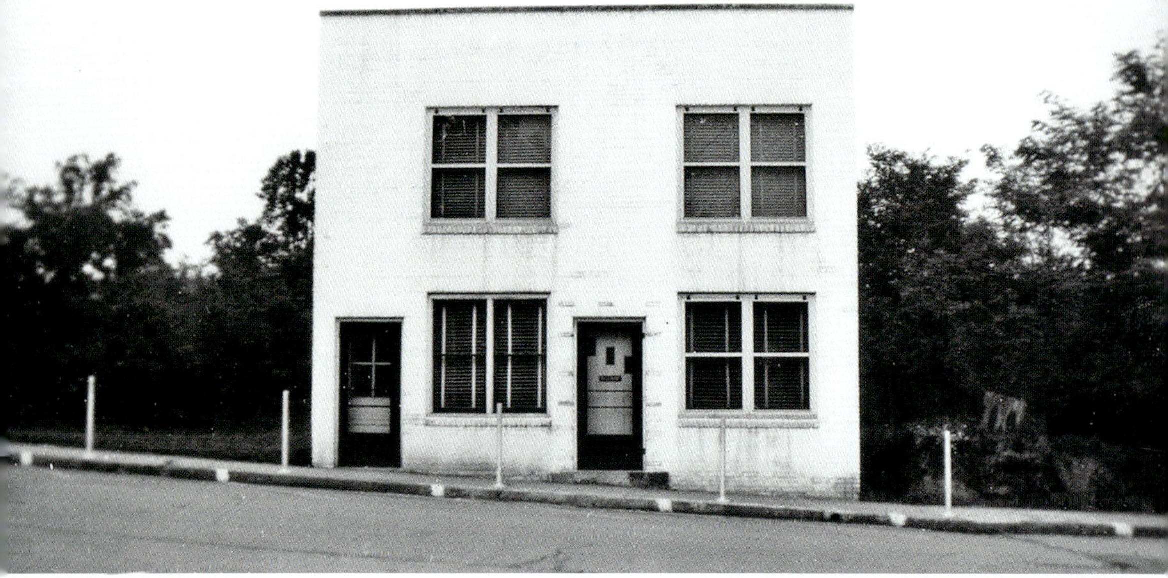

Dr. Ernest J. Anthony's office is shown above in the late 1940s. By June 1946, Dr. Anthony was serving patients from his practice on the first floor. He and his wife, Myrtle, resided upstairs. Between 1946 and 1948, Dr. Anthony hosted a Black Mountain health clinic on Fridays from 9:00 a.m. to noon offering maternity, infancy, and immunization clinics. Dr. Anthony died in mid-1948. Myrtle sold the lots north of the office to George Rankin and Pierre Beeler in 1951, and they built the two adjoining buildings, which are now Doncaster and part of Tyson Furniture. The building is now home to Berliner Kindl German Restaurant.

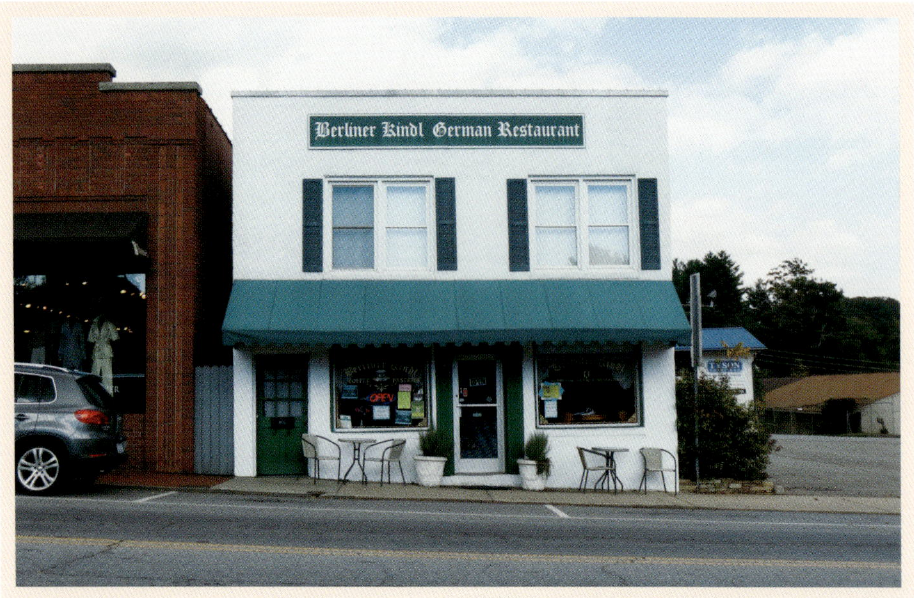

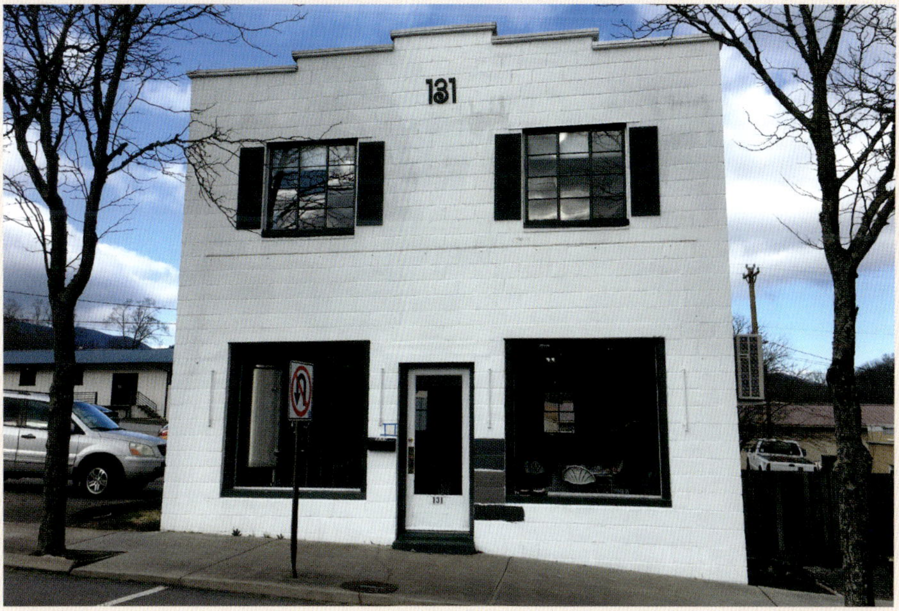

The Wash Spot was built on Broadway Avenue in 1947 by Walter and Dorothy Burgess as a one-story laundromat. The second story was added in 1948. According to a loan the Burgesses acquired from the Swannanoa Bank and Trust Company, the Wash Spot contained nine Bendix washing machines and one water heater. Walter was elected president of the chamber of commerce in 1953, while Dorothy served as vice president of the local woman's club. Most recently, the building served as a prayer room for a short time before being converted to use as a brewery by the owner of Black Mountain Ale House.

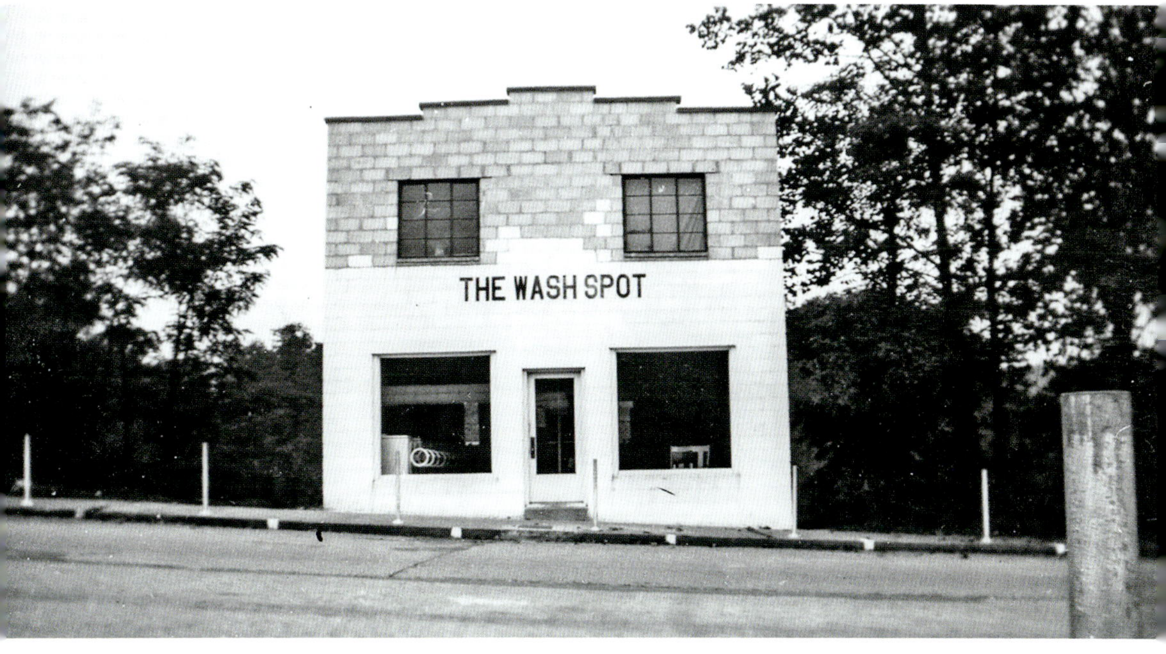

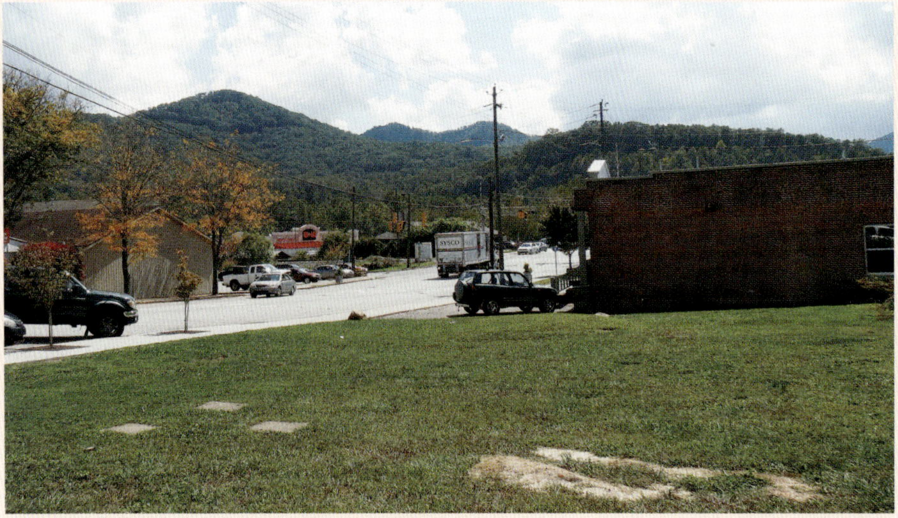

J. Ike Cook, a former employee of Black Mountain Lumber Company, along with B.W. Rowland and Roy A. Taylor, owned Broadway Builders Supply from 1948 until 1958, when they sold the business to the lumber company. When transferring the property and building, Broadway Builders Supply also transferred one Dewalt saw, one jointer, one planer, one typewriter and desk, all shop equipment, and $7,500 in inventory of stock, goods, wares, and merchandise. The lots are now home to Henson Building Materials.

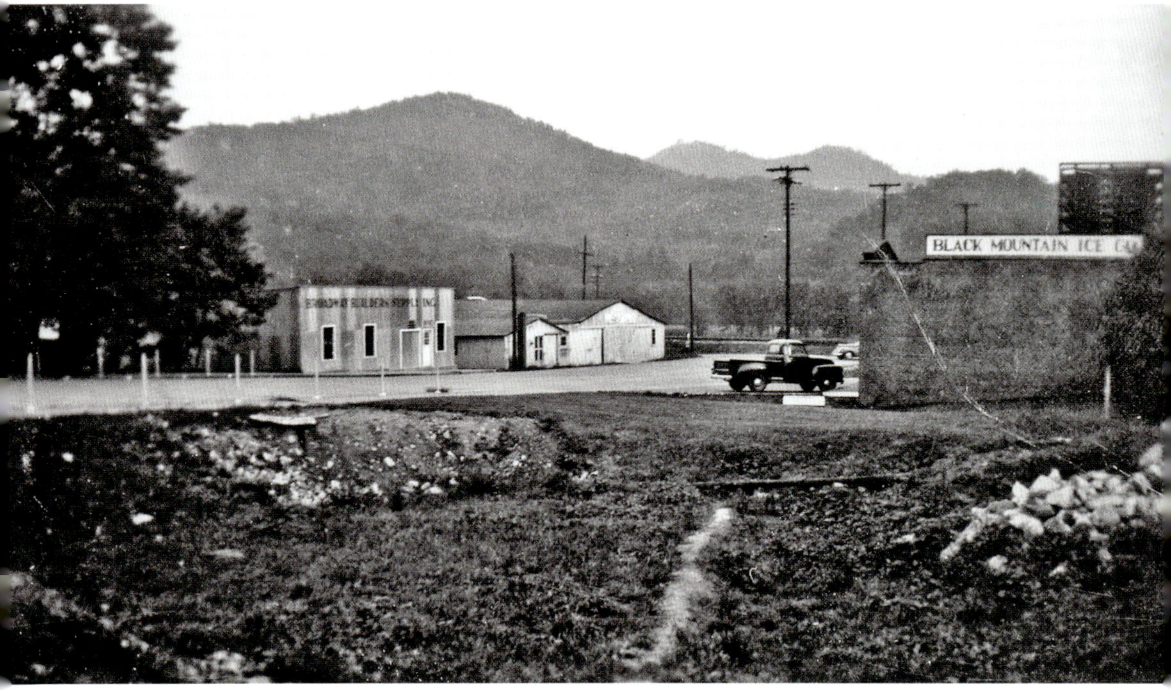

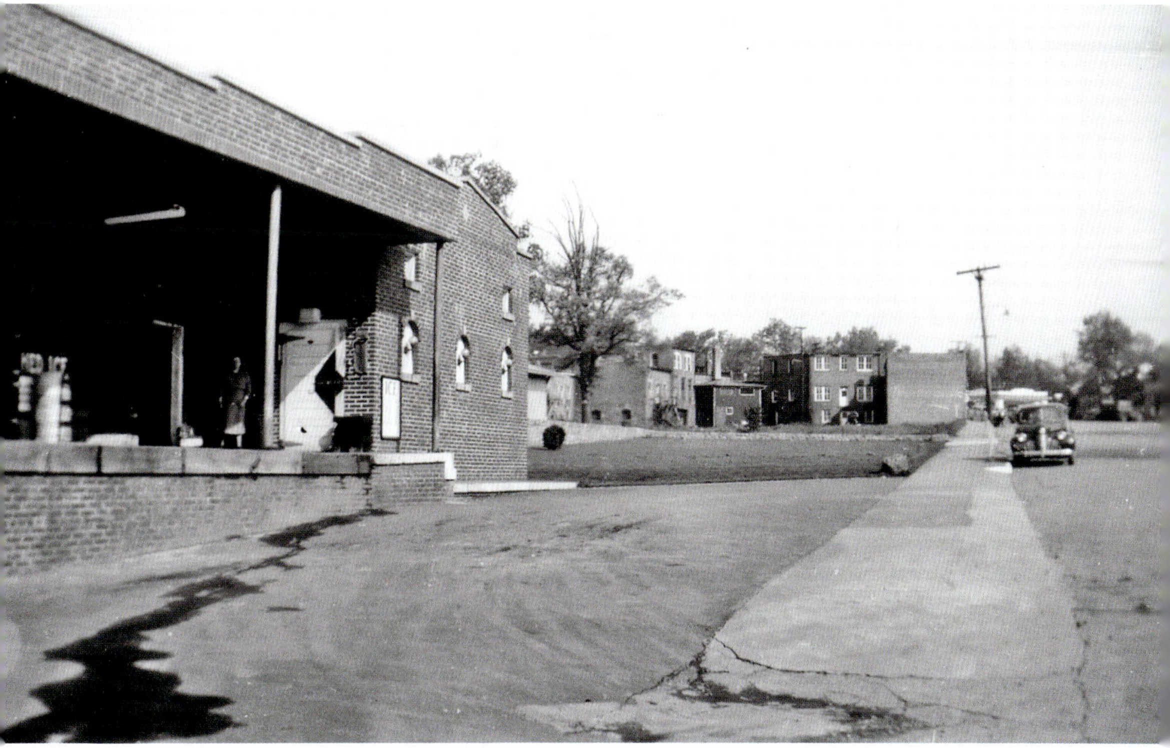

Cyril and Virginia "Jennie" Huffman built the Black Mountain Ice Company, pictured above, around 1930 to manufacture ice and deliver it to area homes. Before the ice company, the lot was home to the original Black Mountain Fire Department (around 1919) as well as the town hall and jail (around 1924). The building has also housed Cook Electric, owned by Worth and Edna Cook, as well as an antique shop, Sourwood Realty, and most recently Gingko Tree Gallery, which closed its doors in 2016. In 2018, the building is slated to be repurposed as a restaurant with rooftop dining.

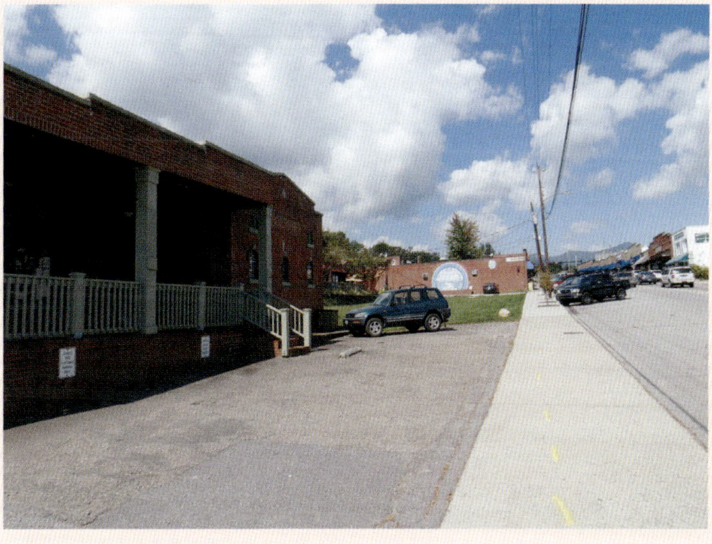

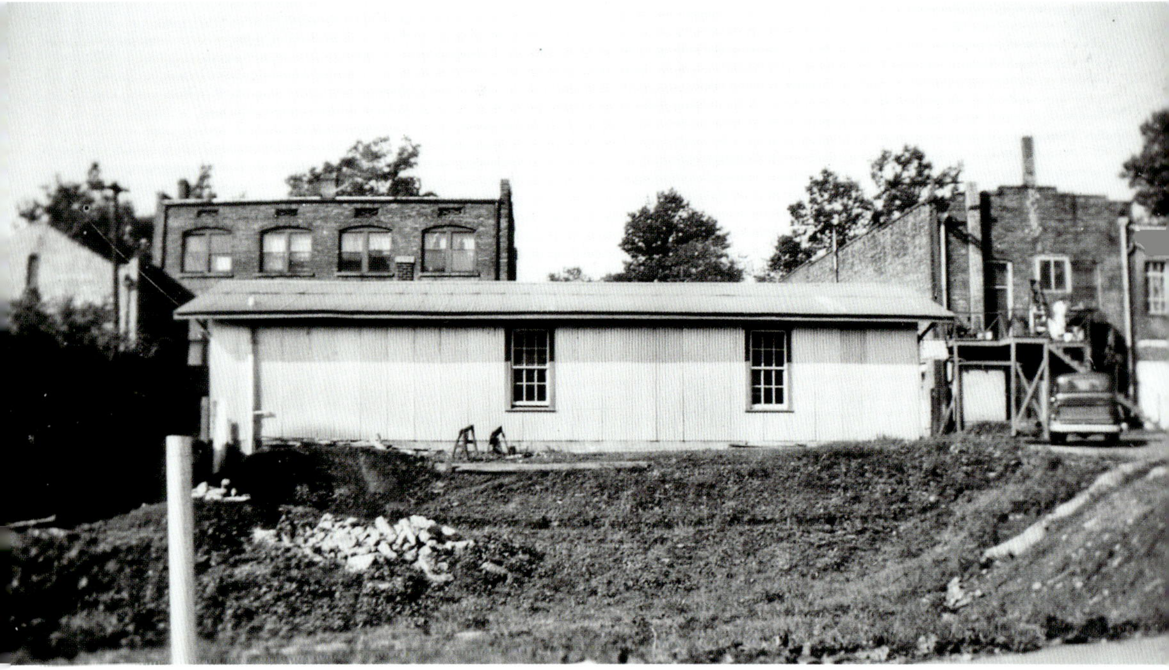

This building was originally constructed as a stable around 1920. It was rebuilt in 1948 by Harry and Kay Hyder as the one-story metal building pictured above. The Hyders were managers of the Western Auto store, which is now Mountain Vista Properties, just north of these photographs. Black Mountain Ice Company later used the building as a garage and coal house. After the death of her husband in 1944, Jennie Huffman married Lee Seagle, and they added an additional commodity: coal. Black Mountain Ice and Coal Company closed in 1959. The building has also housed a metal sculpture workshop, Black Mountain Yoga, and Dobra Tea. It is set to be torn down in 2018 to make room for the three-story Trestle building.

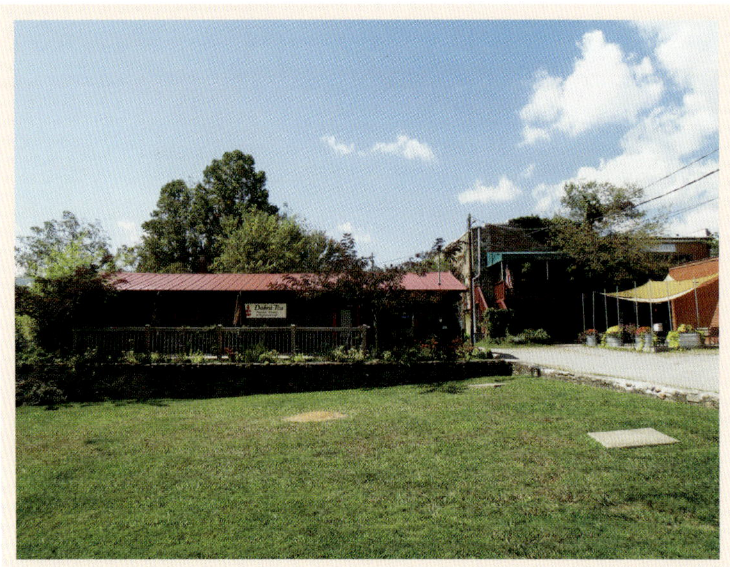

CHAPTER 3

A New Center

State Street

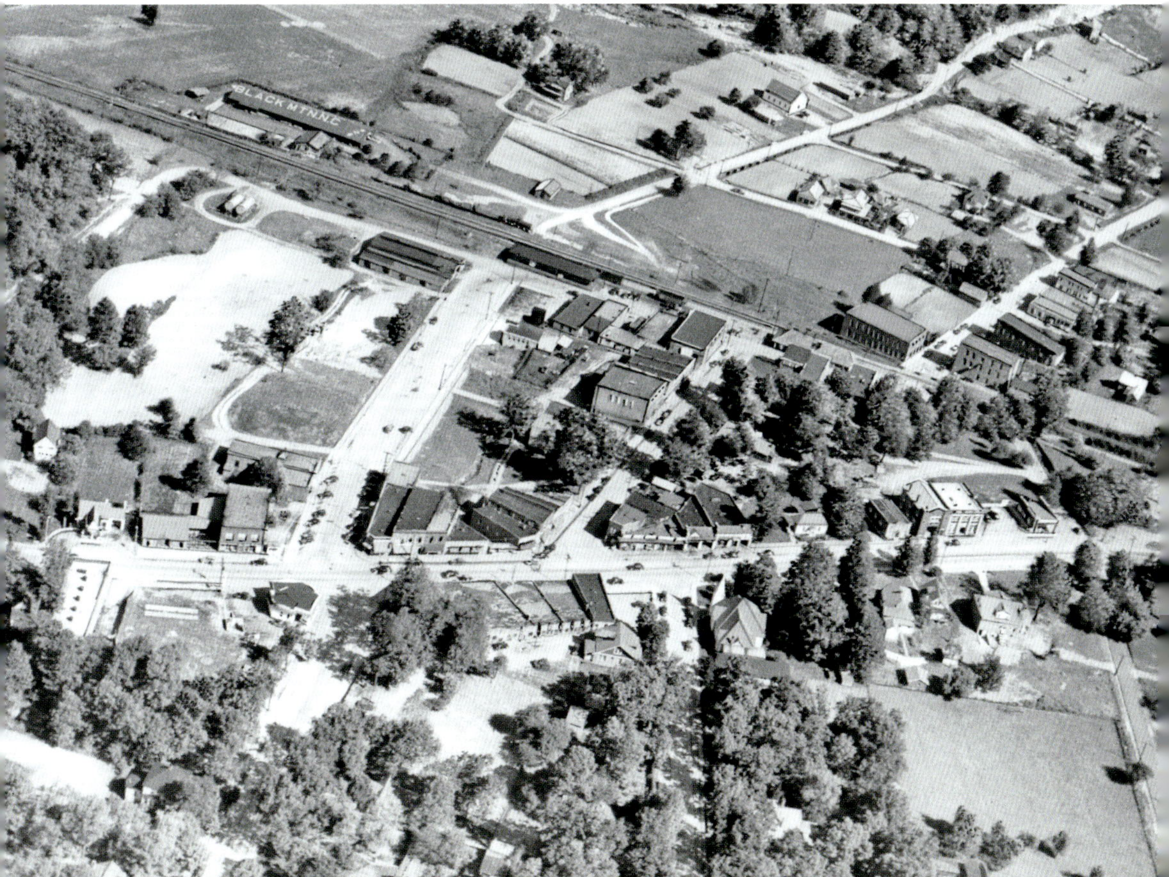

Before the railroad came through Black Mountain, the stagecoach route—now State Street—was the main street through Black Mountain. In the 1880s, the town incorporated and centered around the depot, with development moving north up Cherry Street and Broadway Avenue. In the 1920s, as the automobile became a major mode of transportation, there was a resurgence of development along State Street as it became the major route from Asheville to locations farther east, as can be seen in this c. 1925 aerial view.

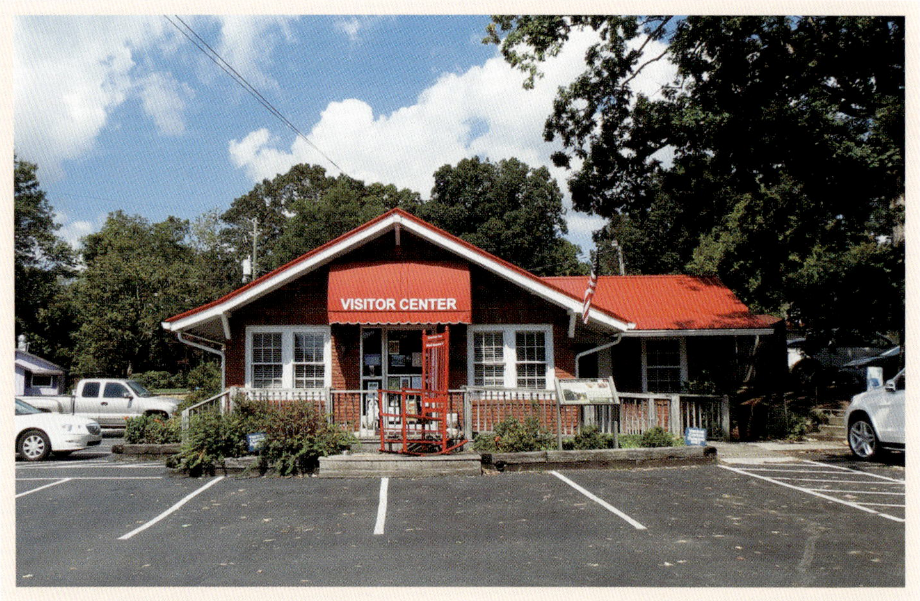

Built in the 1920s by Claudia McGraw and her husband, John, this brick building was originally McGraw's Coffee House. The McGraws served fine food, and people from all over the region would travel to Black Mountain to eat here. Claudia became well-known as an apron maker and later owned and operated a cottage industry out of the building, shipping aprons across the country—including to President Johnson's daughter Lucy. The building also served as the doctor's offices of Dr. Sam Cooley and Dr. H. Rankin Miller and is now the Black Mountain–Swannanoa Chamber of Commerce.

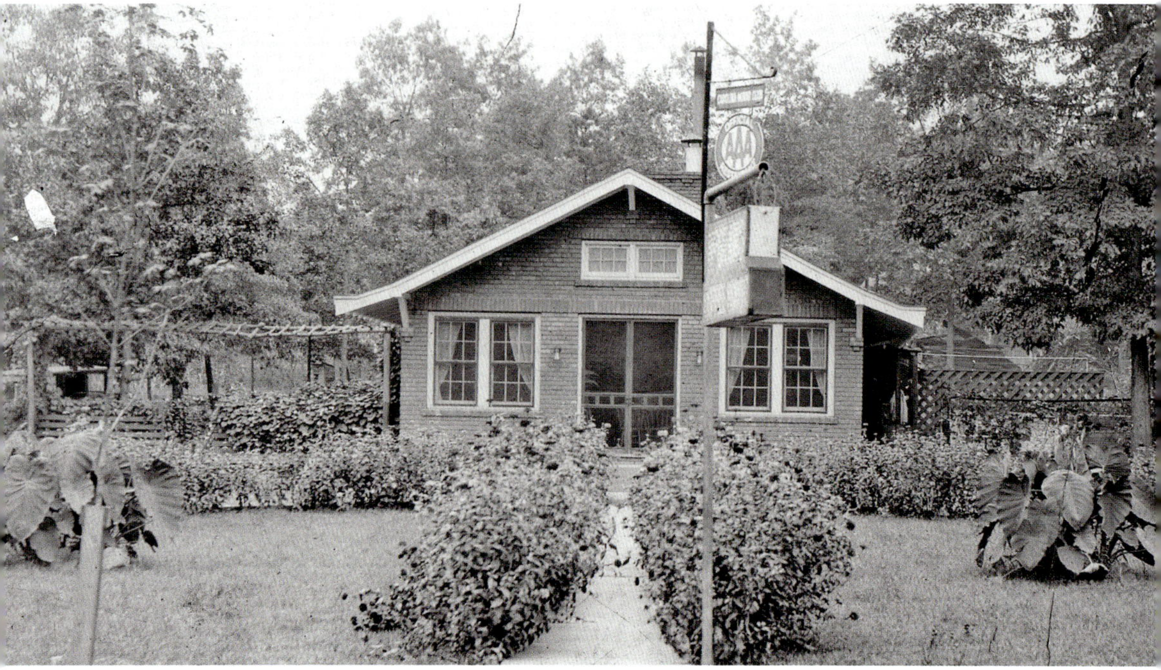

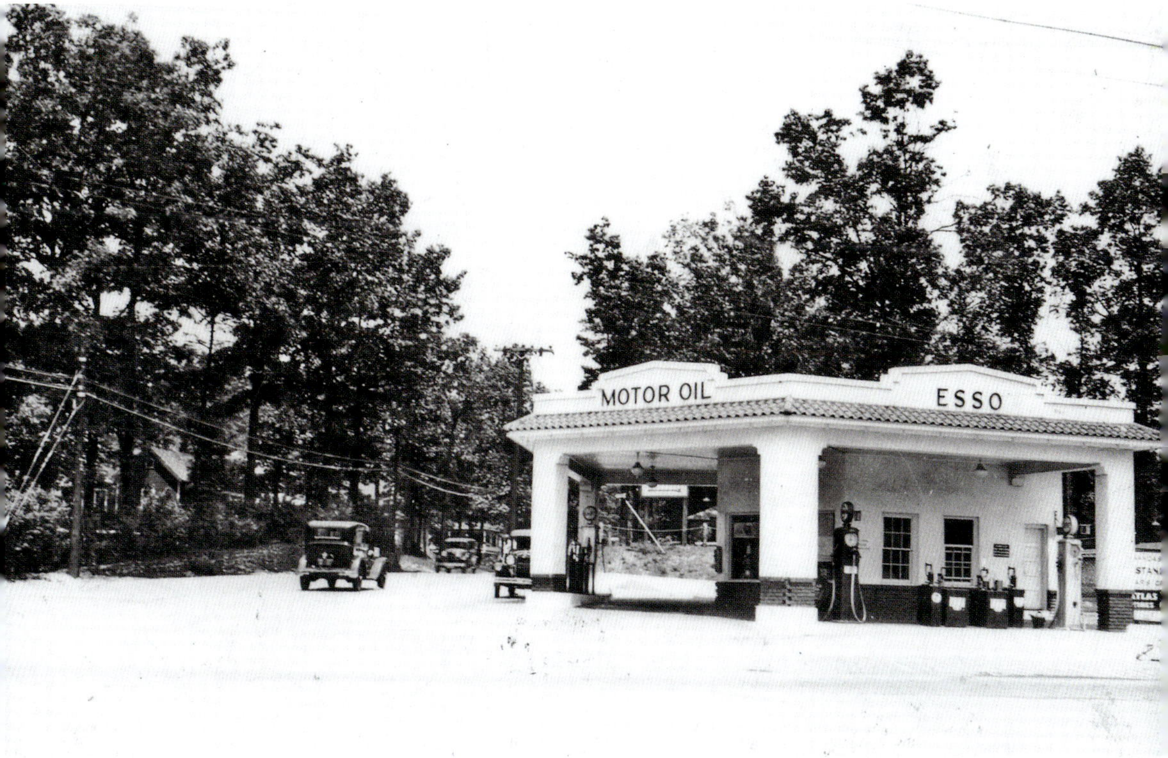

Melvin Lance's Esso station was at the intersection of State Street and Montreat Road, where Town Square is today. The one-room Kerlee School House was also previously at this location. Built around 1923, Lance's Esso station was purchased by James Melvin Lance (1911–1960) in 1930. In 1938, the station boasted clean, modern restrooms for both ladies and gentlemen as well as a complete greasing and oiling service. Until it was torn down in the 2000s, the station continued to sell gasoline.

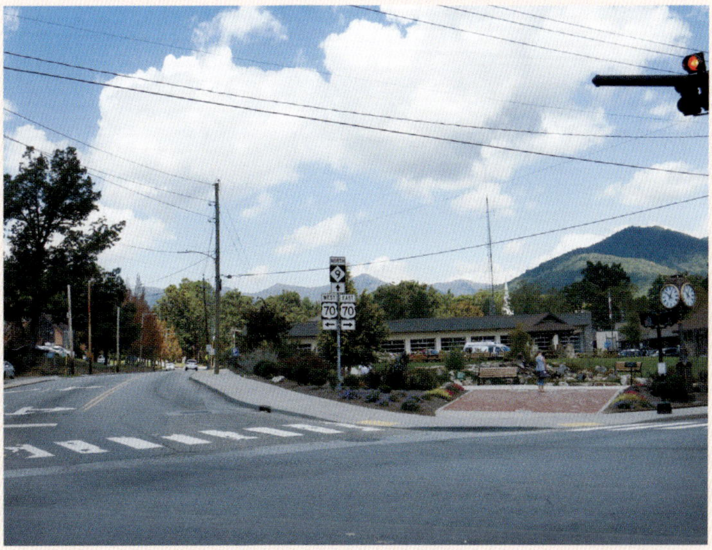

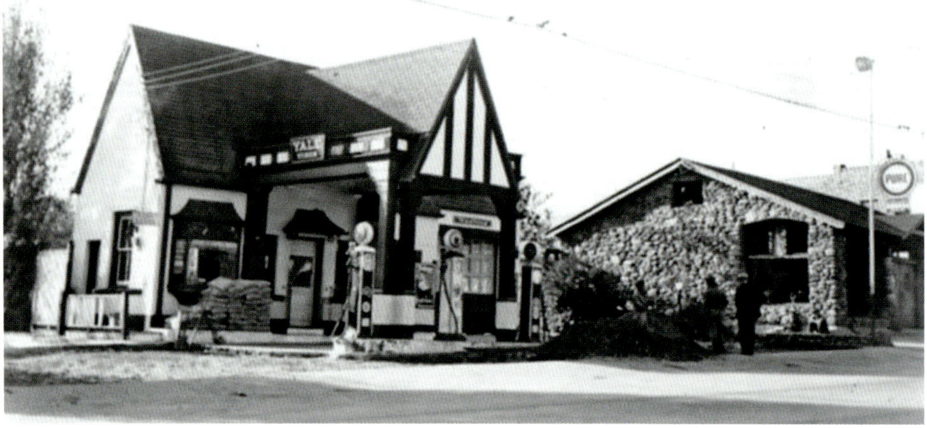

The Pure Oil station was built in the standard "residential" design typical of the 1930s and 1940s, which was meant to comfort drivers. The station was constructed around 1945 by Clyde McElheny and J.G. Macmillan. It was taken over by Ernest and Margaret Slagle. Margaret served as the first female mayor of Black Mountain from 1975 to 1977. A 1975 newspaper article stated, "She works from 8 a.m. until 6 p.m. [at Union station], pumping gasoline or attending to any other jobs at the station including lubrication and minor automobile repair." Just to the west of the station is the Rug and Jug building, constructed in 1934 by Marius E. Rondel. The store, which sold crafts, gifts, and novelties, including wooden toys made by Rondel, was gutted by fire in 1968 but rebuilt. Rondel continued to run the store until he retired in 1971. Both buildings are now owned by Tyson Furniture.

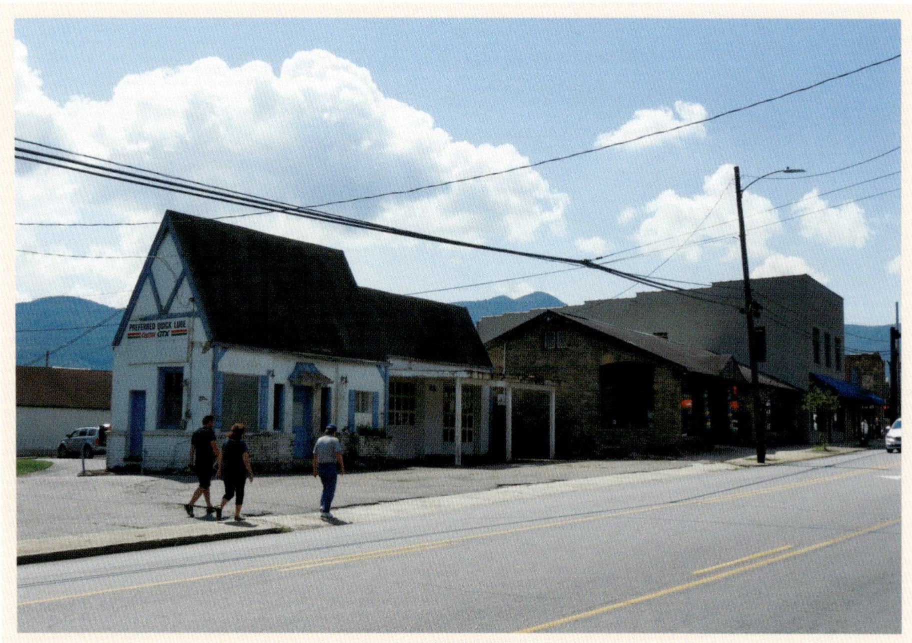

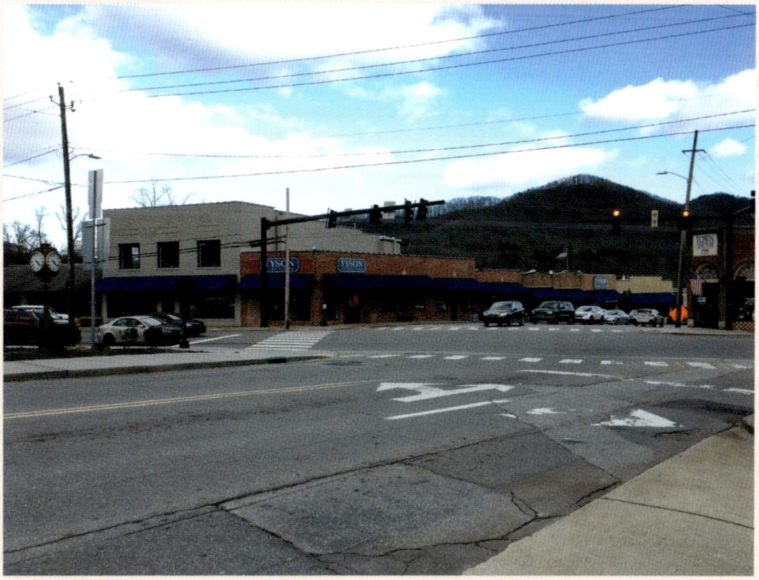

Montreat Road is pictured where it intersects with State Street and becomes Broadway Avenue. The Reed's Café building, with the Coca-Cola advertisement, was built around 1925 for R.H. "Harley" Reed's grocery store. In the 1940s, he converted the building to Reed's Café. At this time, he and his family lived on the second floor and let rooms to boarders. Next door, the bowling alley was built in 1927 by local developer Valentine Avena. According to a 1944 lawsuit taken out by Reed, the bowling alley was a nuisance because it was open-air and operated at night. Later, it was replaced by the brick building that still stands today and became a men's clothing store. Both buildings are now part of Tyson Furniture.

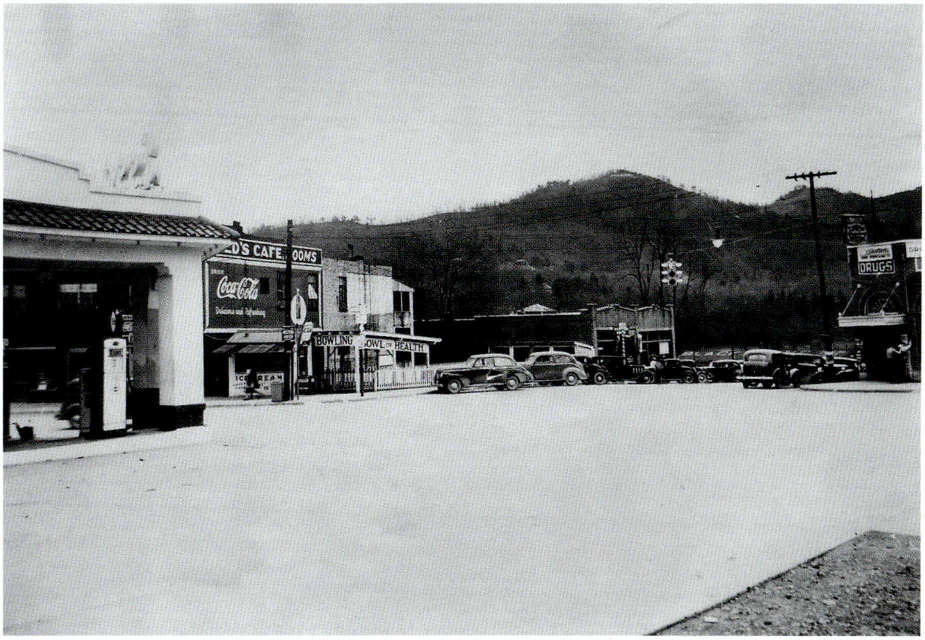

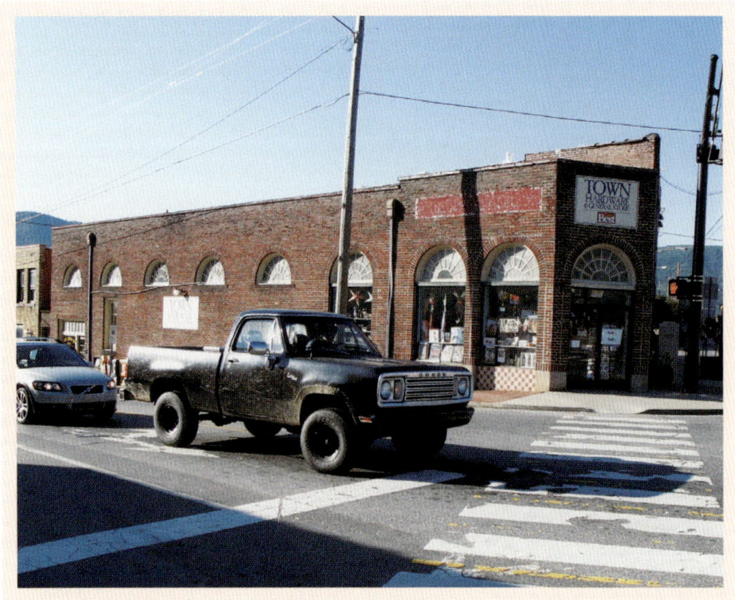

In 1913, Clifford C. Porter moved from Concord to Black Mountain to charter Black Mountain Drug Company with E.W. White and Albert J. Terrell on Sutton Avenue. They purchased their initial stock of drugs from Swannanoa Pharmacy, which had been on the corner of Sutton Avenue and Cherry Street. They also served foods and drinks, carried candy and souvenirs, and sold liquor and tobacco products. In 1928, Porter moved to his new building at the corner of Broadway Avenue and State Street, pictured here, which now houses Town Hardware & General Store. Though the drugstore changed names and owners through the years, it operated as a pharmacy and soda fountain until 1999. (Now photograph by Craig Cooley.)

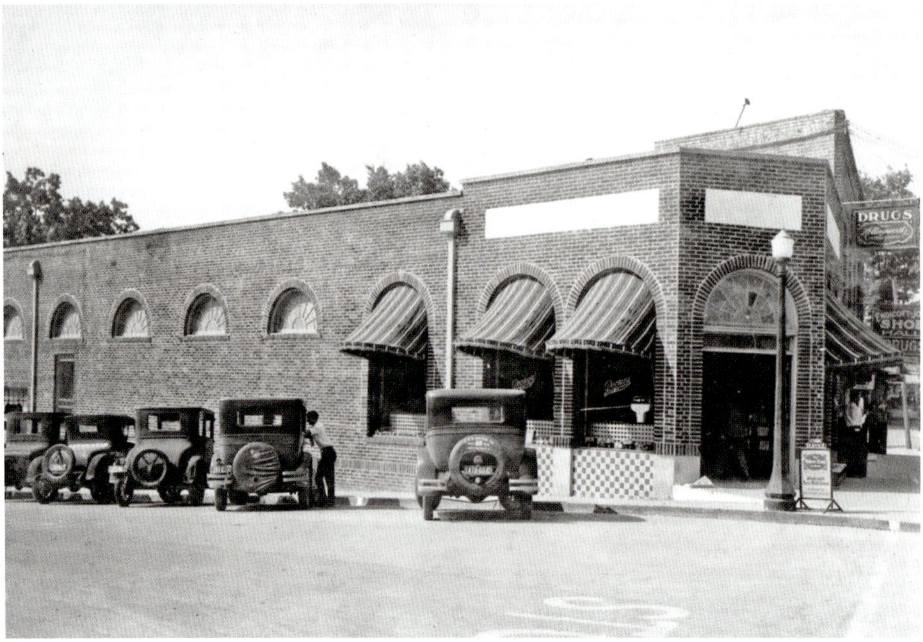

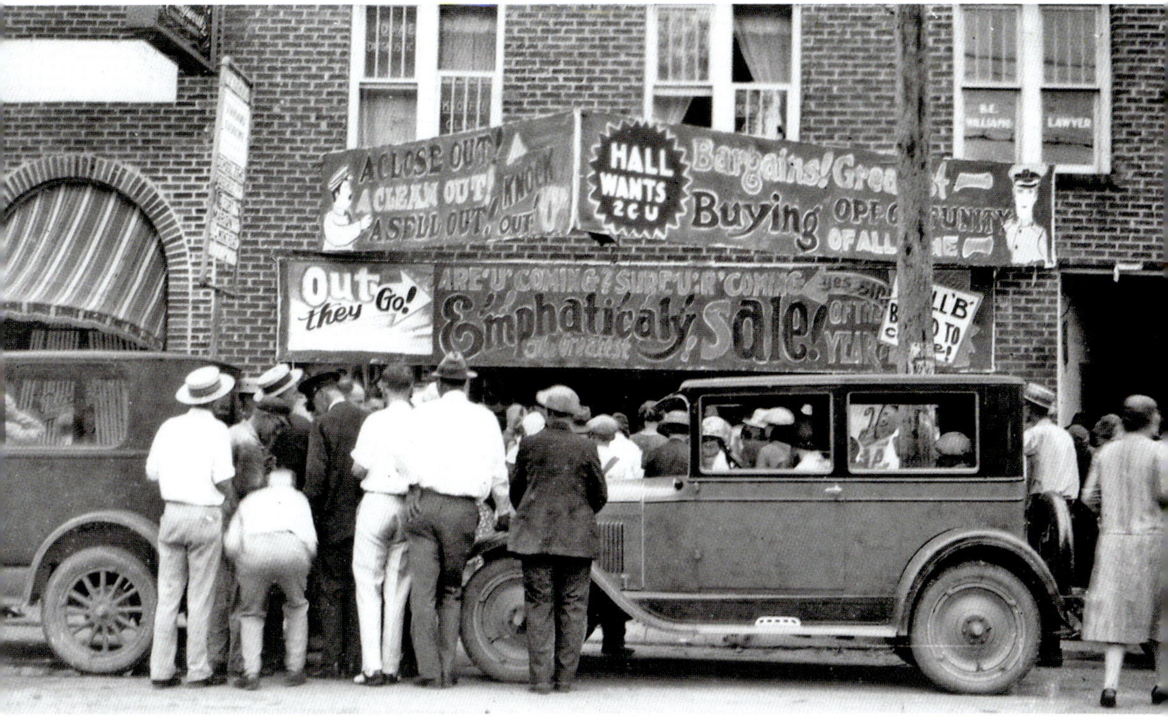

Black Mountain Hardware & Supply Company was a fixture in Black Mountain since at least the 1910s. Started by Robert Lee Woodard in a storefront on Sutton Avenue, the company was officially incorporated in 1926. In 1934, the hardware store moved from the corner of State and Cherry Streets to the Howerton building on State Street (pictured here), leasing the basement and first floor. In the 1960s, the hardware store relocated, and Archie Wolf opened Town Hardware in the building. In 1999, with the closing of the Black Mountain Drug Company, Town Hardware expanded.

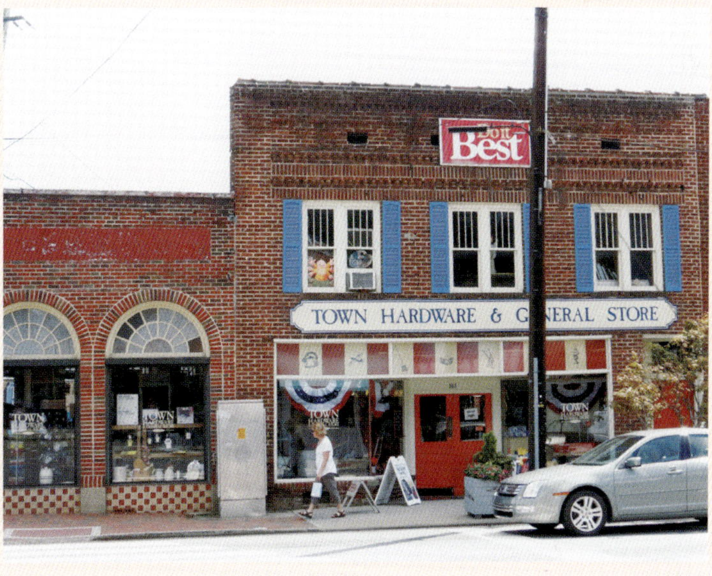

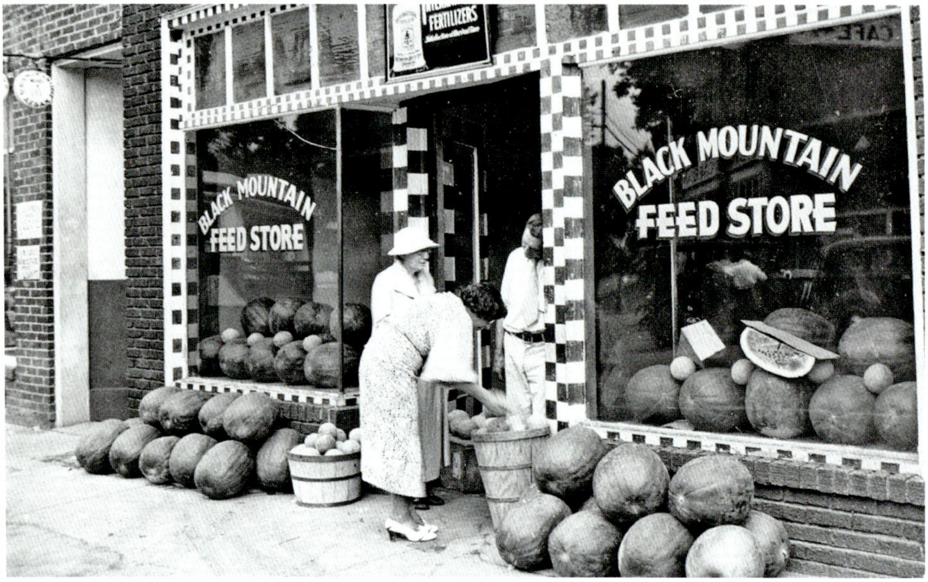

Now part of Town Hardware & General Store, the Black Mountain Feed Store was constructed in the early 1920s. Early on, it was used as a grocery store by Tom Miller. From 1935 until 1964, J.L. Pence operated Pence's, a five-and-dime store, here. Before the building to the right of Pence's was constructed around 1930, a service station operated on the site. Built to house G&H Trucking, which delivered food and other goods to A&P groceries, it changed hands in the 1930s, when Roger Viverette and his wife, Minnie Woodard Viverette, purchased the land and building from her parents, Robert and Maggie Woodard. Roger opened Viverette's radio sales and repair in the building.

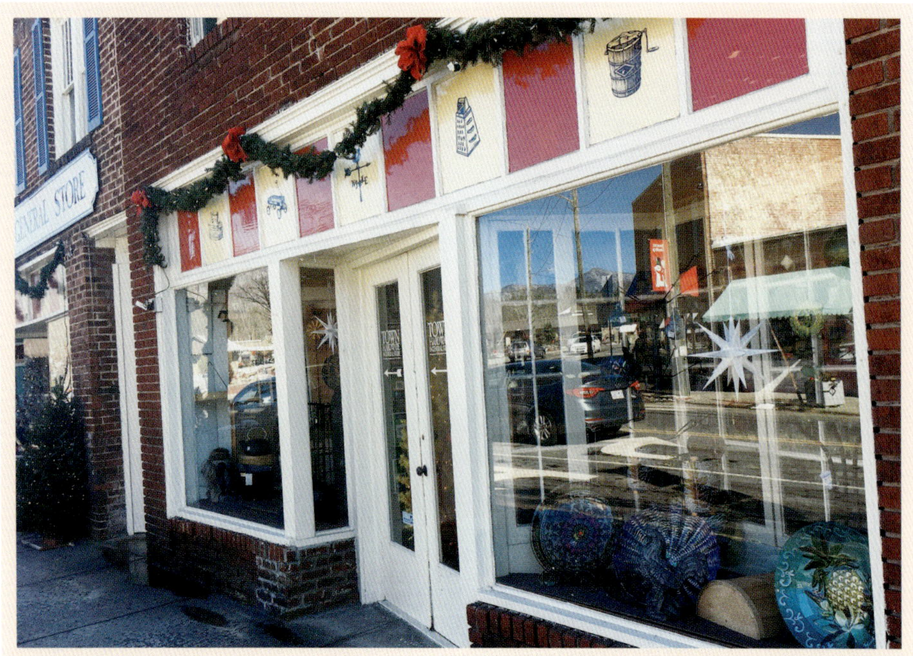

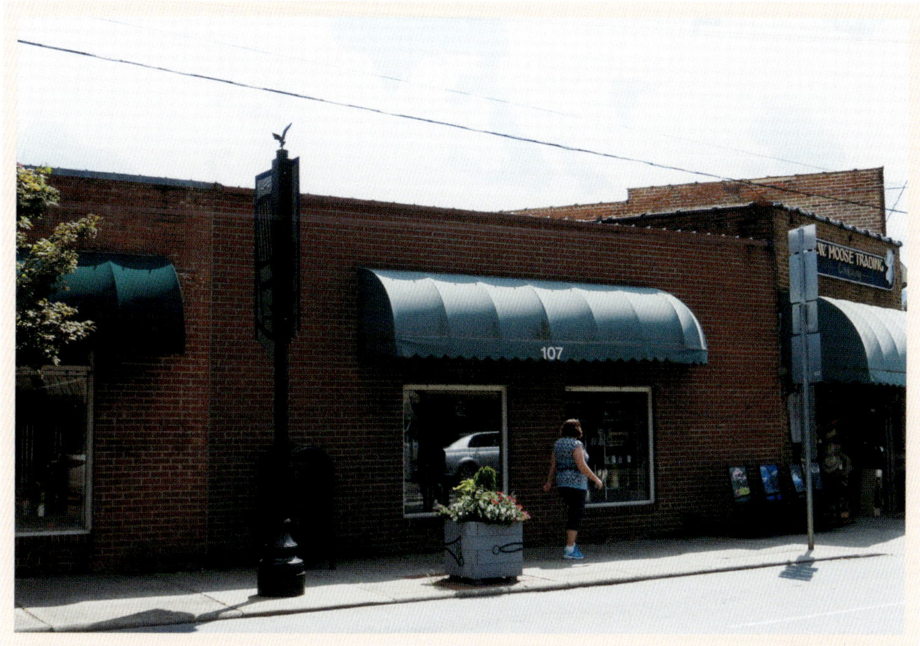

The photograph below, taken in 1956 by Edward DuPuy, shows a large tourist map that was located on State Street between present-day Brandon's and C.W. Moose Trading Company. In the 1990s, the Brandons built an addition to their building where the map is. This was also the former location of an honor roll erected by the Lion's Club listing all of Black Mountain's veterans. To the right of the map, what is now Moose Trading Company was once Albert Garland's restaurant and eventually became The Grill.

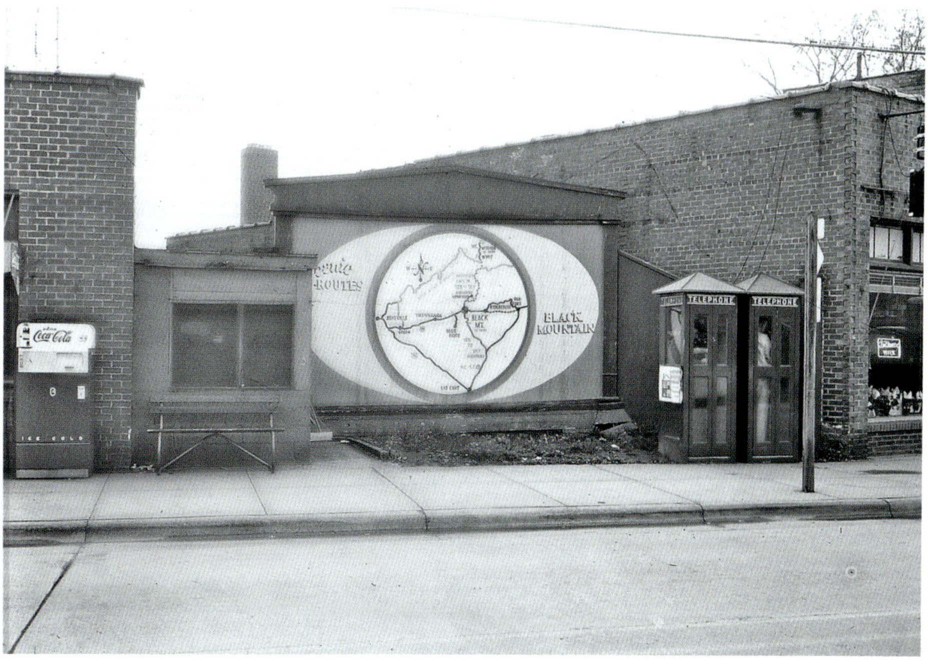

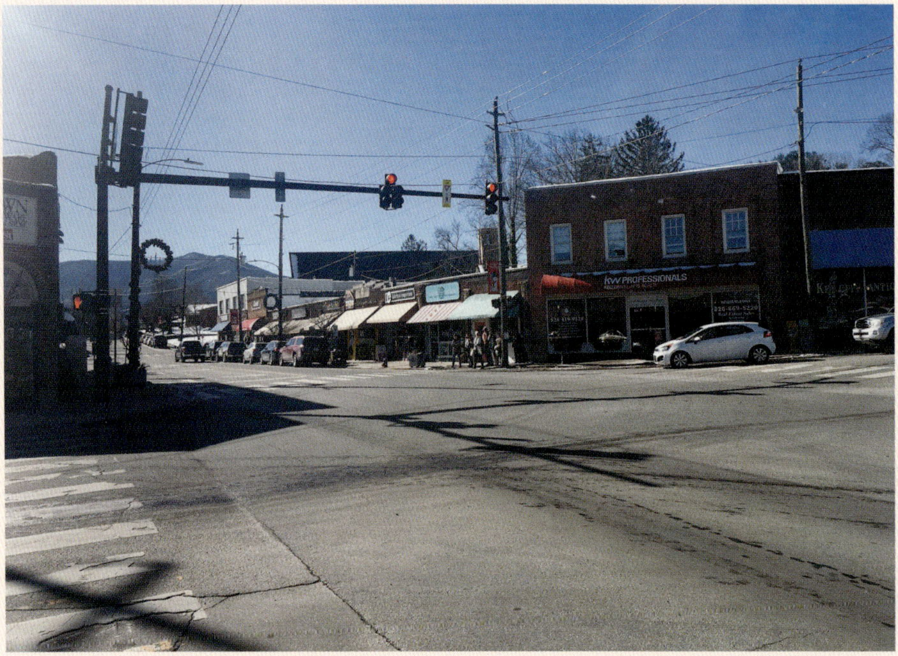

The American Café was built 1923 as an auto shop. It became the Black Mountain Garage in the late 1920s. The Ingles family operated an American Café in Black Mountain as early as the 1910s, but the building pictured here did not become the American Café until at least the 1930s. By 1950, the building became the Dixie Home Store, a grocery that merged with Winn and Lovett to become the Winn-Dixie grocery chain in 1956. It is now home to Keller Williams Realty.

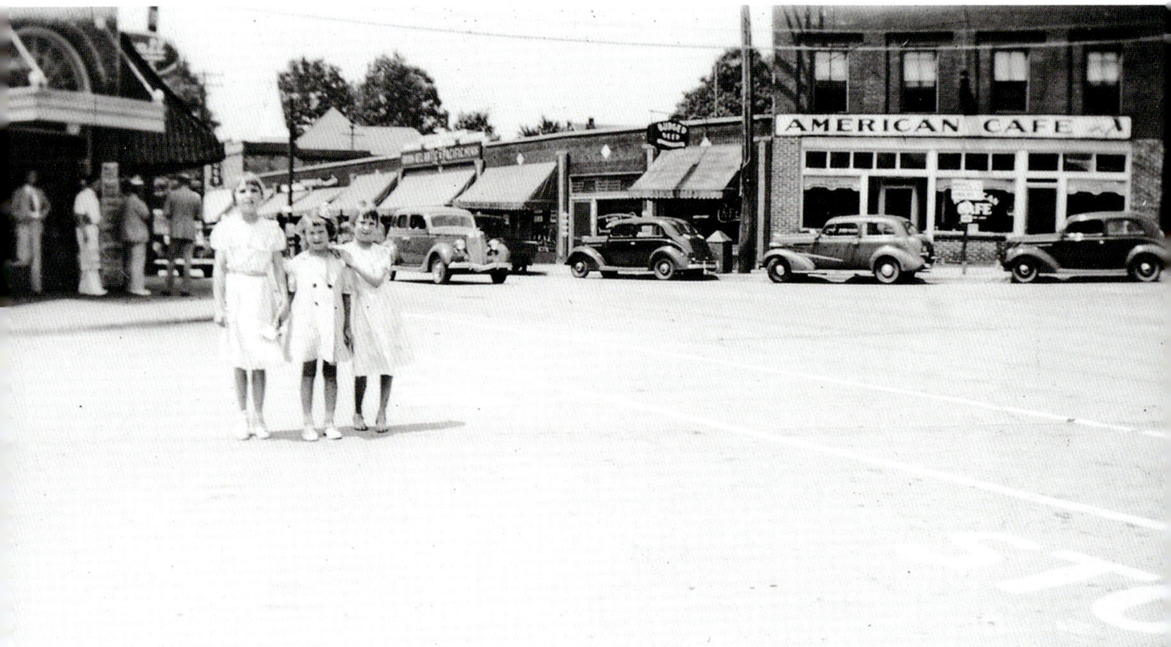

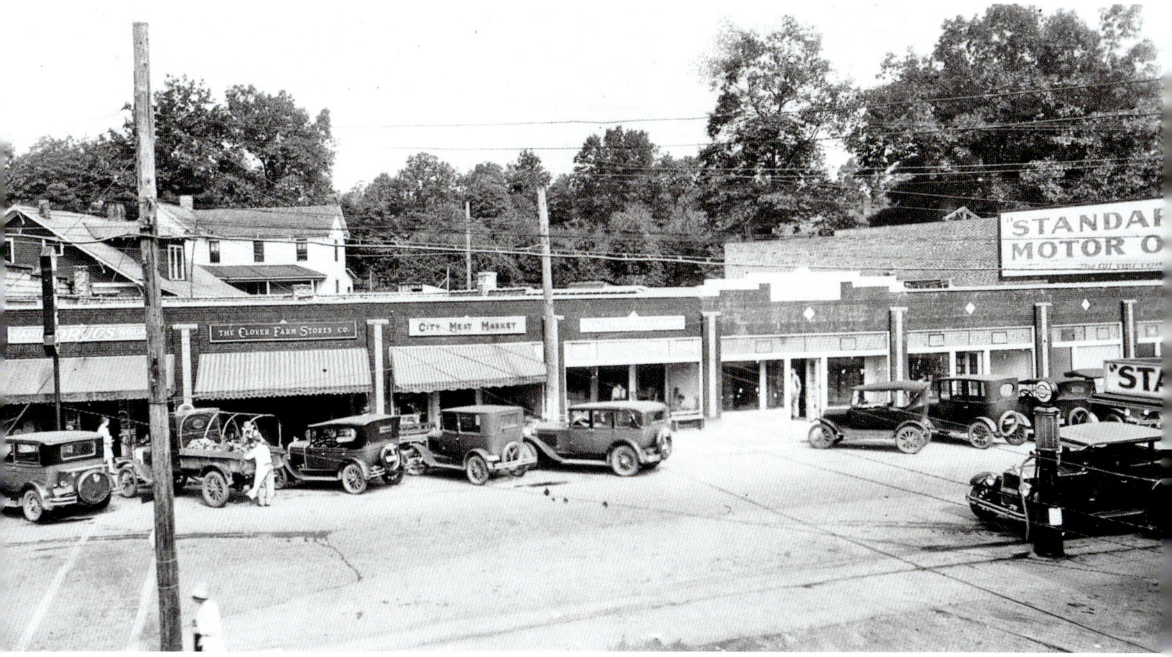

Along the north side of West State Street is the Kaltman building, a series of eight similar storefronts constructed in 1928 by Samuel Kaltman, a clothing manufacturer from New York who came to the area in 1921 for his health. By 1926, along with his wife, Bessie, he was a leading developer in Black Mountain, controlling about half of the real estate in the downtown business section. Besides the Kaltman building, he also built a garage and store at the corner of State and Cherry Streets. Kaltman died of a stroke in 1938 in his shop on Church Street where he made men's trousers. These storefronts have been home to a wide variety of businesses since their construction, including a drugstore, hardware store, grocery, meat market, tea company, barbershop, cupcake shop, wine market, and running store.

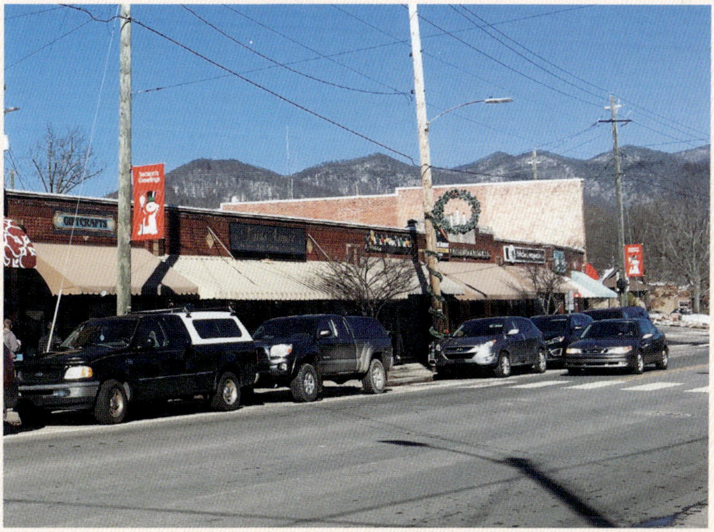

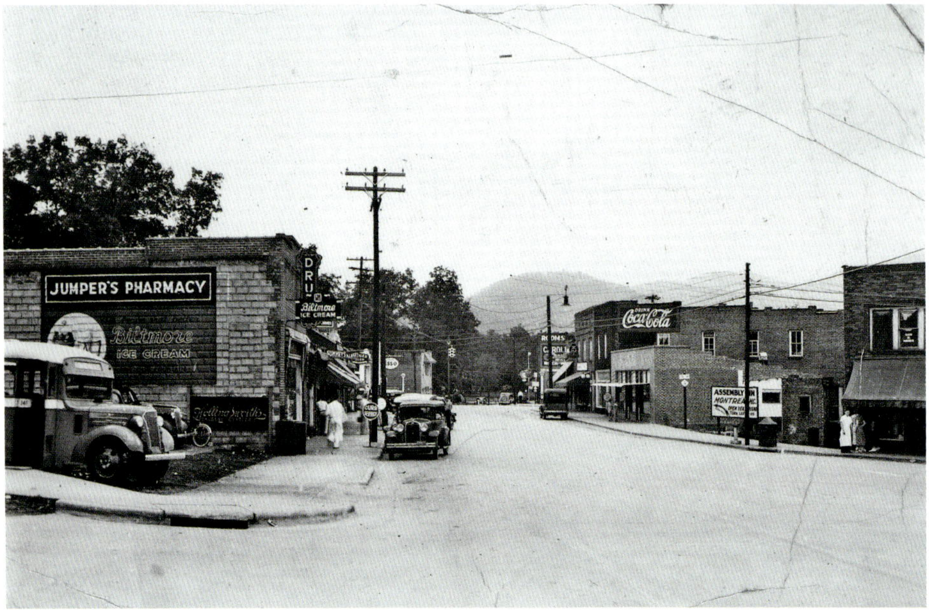

The Victory Theatre was officially chartered in 1919. Will Sharp operated the theater until 1921, when he suffered a breakdown and his nephew Gerald took over operations. Sometime prior to 1924, the theater closed. In July 1924, Lee Hiltz, who was in the process of building a new, modern theater on East State Street, reopened the Victory until work on his theater was complete. In 1925, due to the widening of State Street, the building's original facade was demolished and the storefront moved farther from the road. Around this time, the building was adapted for use as a pharmacy by Dr. L. Clyde Jumper, who continued as proprietor until 1945, when he sold the building to Edward Hines Knight. Knight operated the pharmacy with his wife, Ruby, for over 30 years. It is now Kilwin's.

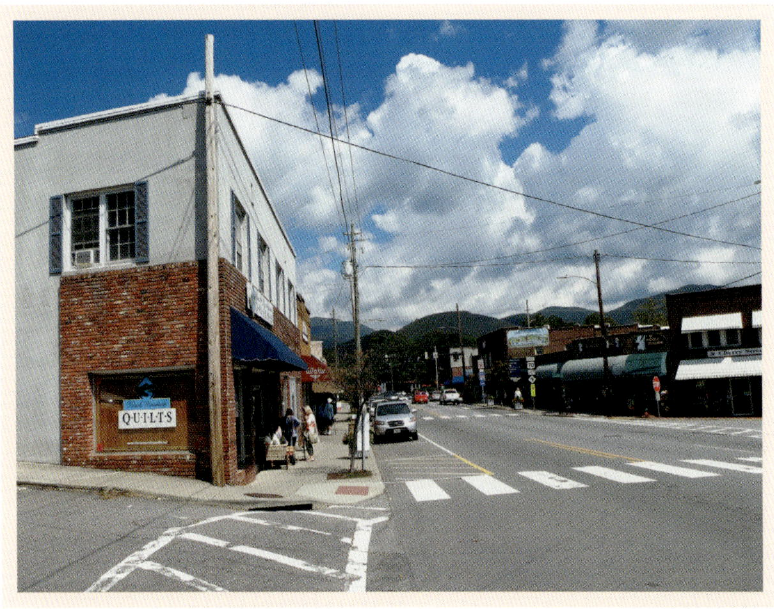

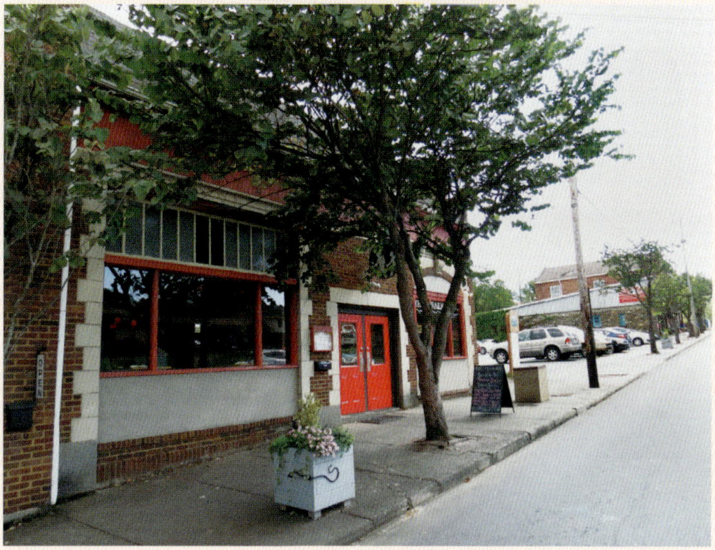

Before I-40, the main route travelers took to get east came down State Street. As one of the last stops before Old Fort, this thoroughfare contained a host of filling stations, repair centers, and auto dealerships. One of the most notable was McMurray Chevrolet Company, seen in the 1954 Edward DuPuy photograph below. The building was constructed in 1927 for a Chevrolet dealership that went bankrupt during the Depression. William H. McMurray Sr. bought the building and operated his dealership here beginning in 1935, when the cars would arrive on the train, four to a boxcar. Eventually, McMurray's son and grandson took over the business. The building is now home to the Trailhead Restaurant, and the car lot next door is a public parking lot.

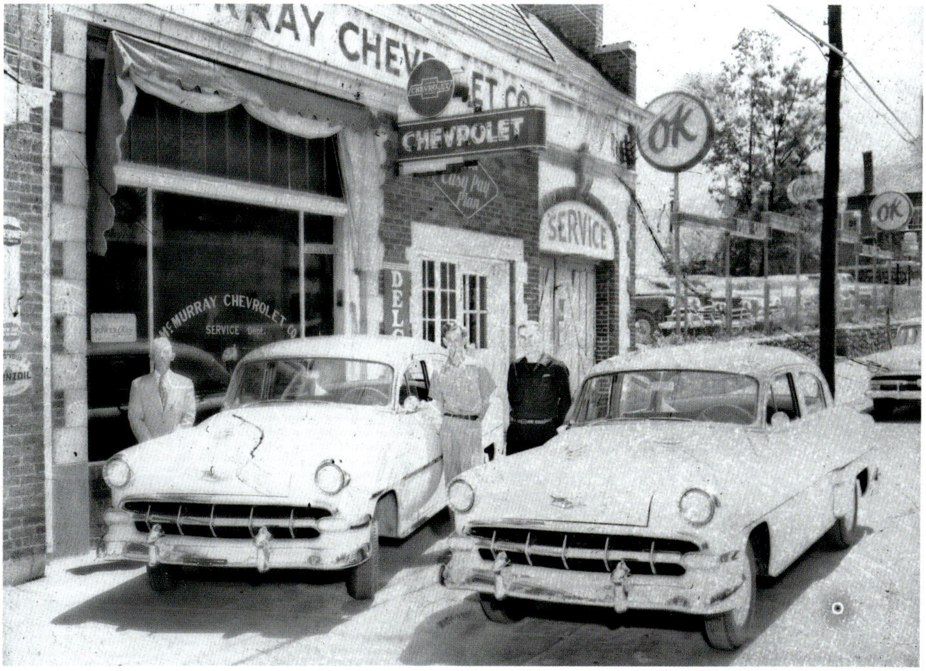

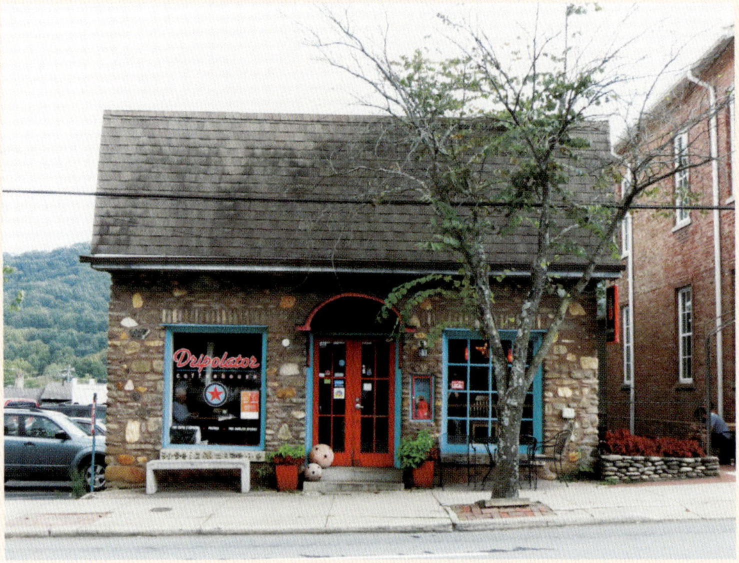

The river-rock building that now houses the Dripolator Coffeehouse was built in late 1929 by local photographer Walter Bingham Gragg as his studio and business. Several of his photographs appear in this book. In the 1940s, the building became a beauty shop managed by Lora Hamby Reed. In the late 1950s, the shop was known as Bea's Beauty Shop and Gifts, operated by Bea Glover. Though unsubstantiated, a favorite local legend is that the building also housed a funeral home at one time. As the story goes, what is now the alleyway between the Dripolator and the Swannanoa Valley Museum was open to one-way automobile traffic, and the large picture window on the west side of the building was used as a drive-by viewing window.

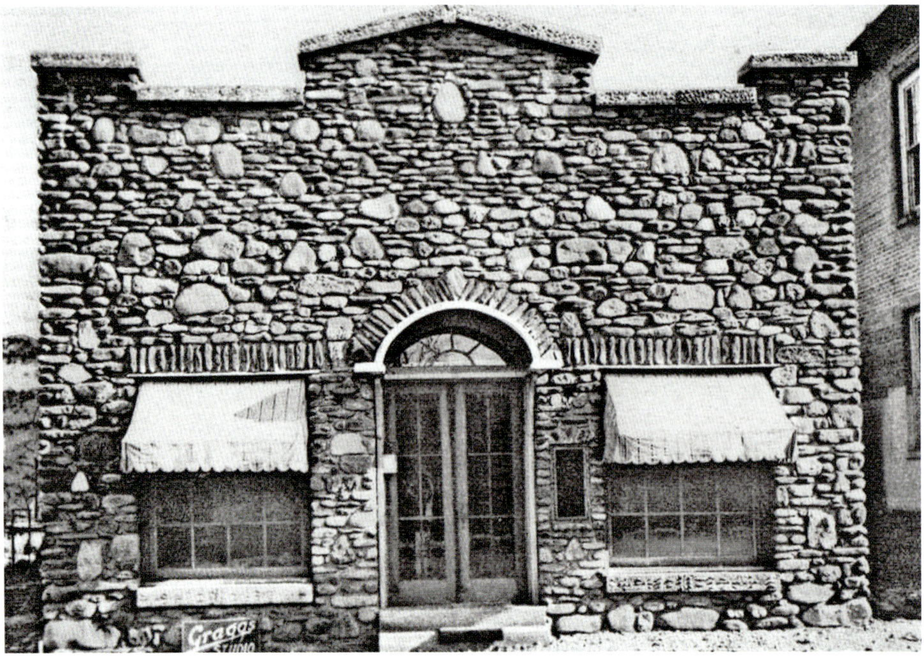

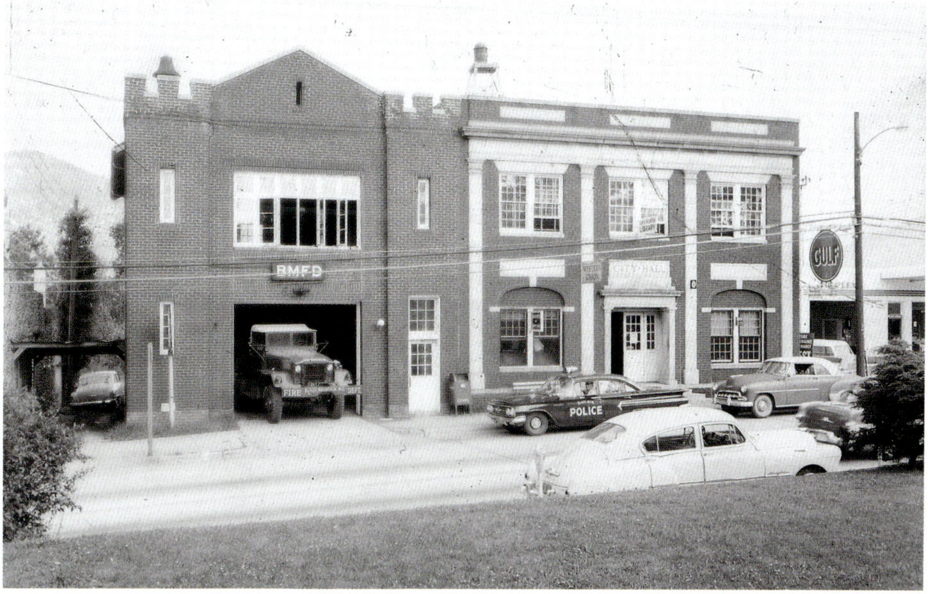

After the 1912 fire destroyed much of downtown, concerned citizens organized a fire department. By 1919, the first fire station was erected on the northwest corner of Broadway and Sutton Avenues. In 1922, the fire department relocated to Currier Hall (named after fire chief Robert E. Currier), pictured around 1960 in the Edward DuPuy photograph above. The two-story brick building, designed in 1921 by Biltmore Estate supervising architect Richard Sharp Smith, was the inspiration for the multitude of brick-front businesses built downtown over the next century. The department moved to its present location in 1984, and this building has been home to the Swannanoa Valley Museum since 1989. In 1927, the town hall was built adjoining the firehouse. Home to the Black Mountain Center for the Arts since 2000, the town hall has also served as the police department, the library from 1927 to 1968, the jail until 1971, the chamber of commerce, a Western Union telegraph office, and a courtroom.

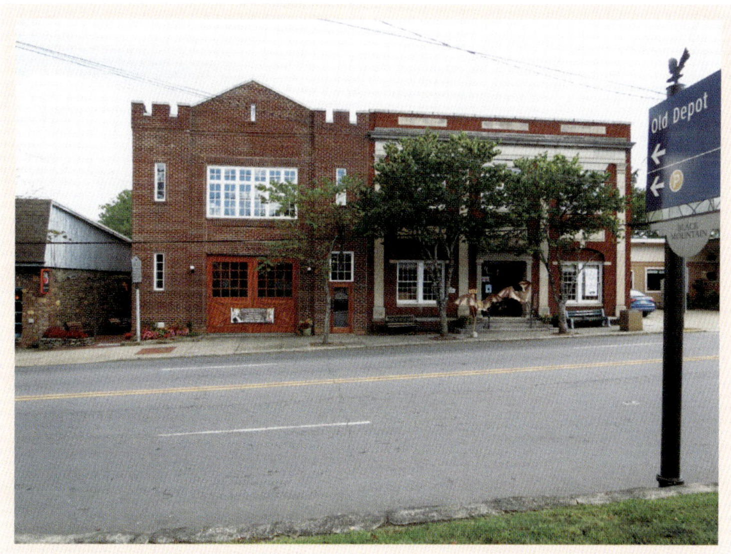

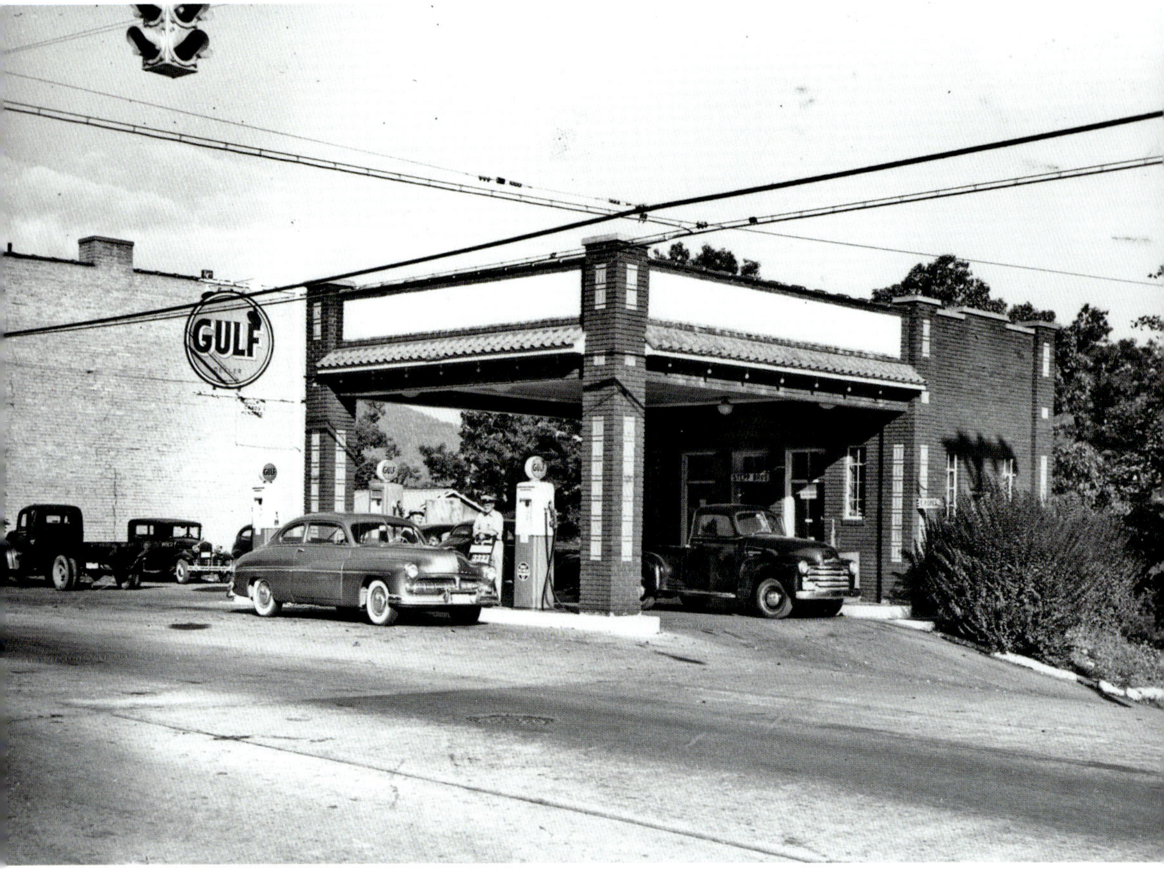

In 1954, the Stepp Brothers Gulf station opened at the corner of State and Dougherty Streets in the present location of Thai Basil. The photograph above by W.B. Gragg shows owners Roy B. Stepp and his brother in front of the pumps. At the same time, a station owned by J.O. Williams selling Gulf products was being constructed on the other end of State Street to the east of the Pix Theatre.

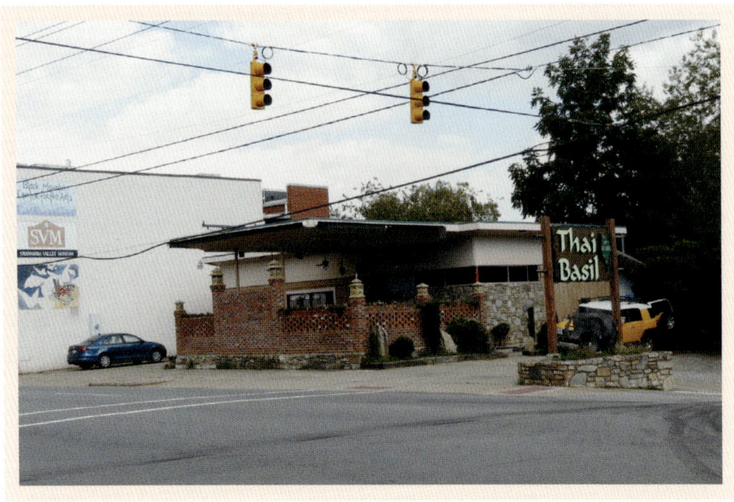

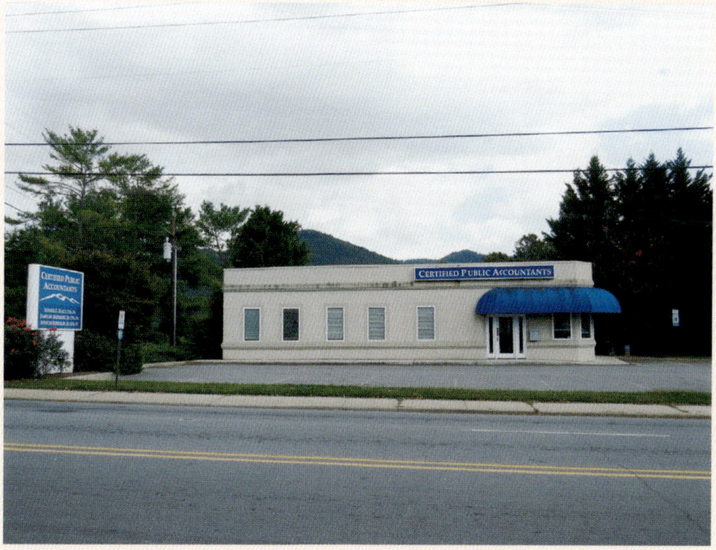

In 1953, J. Max Woodcock leased the site of his former filling station to Esso to build a new, modern, two-bay service station with concrete drives, porcelain enamel facades, floodlights, and a drive-on auto lift. By 1954, Austin Burgess had opened it as Burgess' Esso Service Center. In 1964, Wade Shook Jr. incorporated Black Mountain Esso and took over operations. Three years later, he leased the adjacent property to the west to operate a car-wash. The much-renovated building now houses the certified public accountant offices of Ronnie G. Seals, James M. Skidmore, and Spencer Robinson Jr.

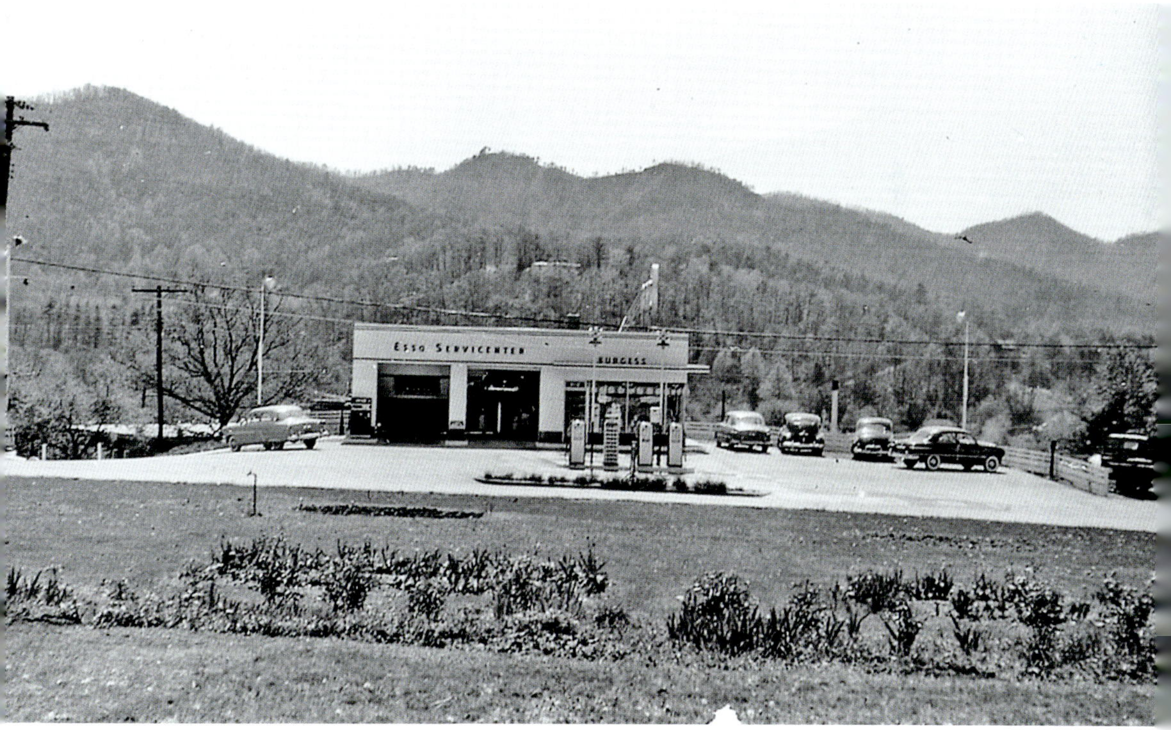

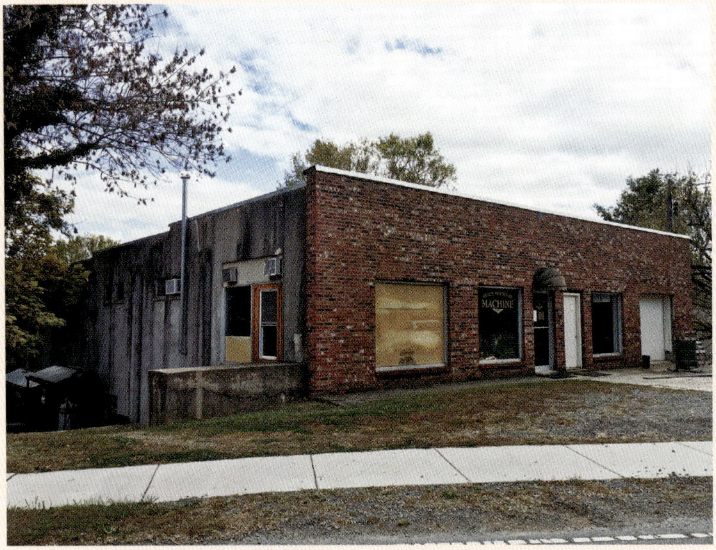

Black Mountain Super Market and Freezer Lockers, on Montreat Road in the present location of Black Mountain Machine and Tool's corporate offices, broke ground in April 1948. The first self-service grocery in town, it also offered meat processing and curing rooms as well as bulk storage for fruits and vegetables on the ground floor. Shaw's Store leased the far left portion of the top floor, pictured below, as a gift shop. Before residents began purchasing home freezers in the mid-1950s, freezer lockers were in high demand, and when the business officially opened in December 1948, most of the freezer lockers had already been rented for $12.50 to $16.50 annually.

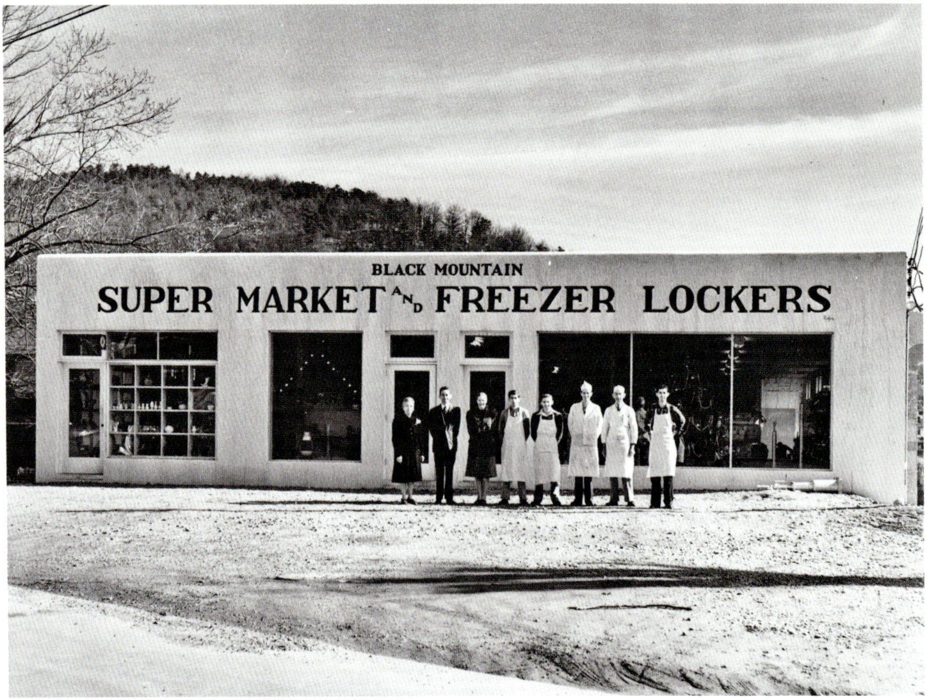

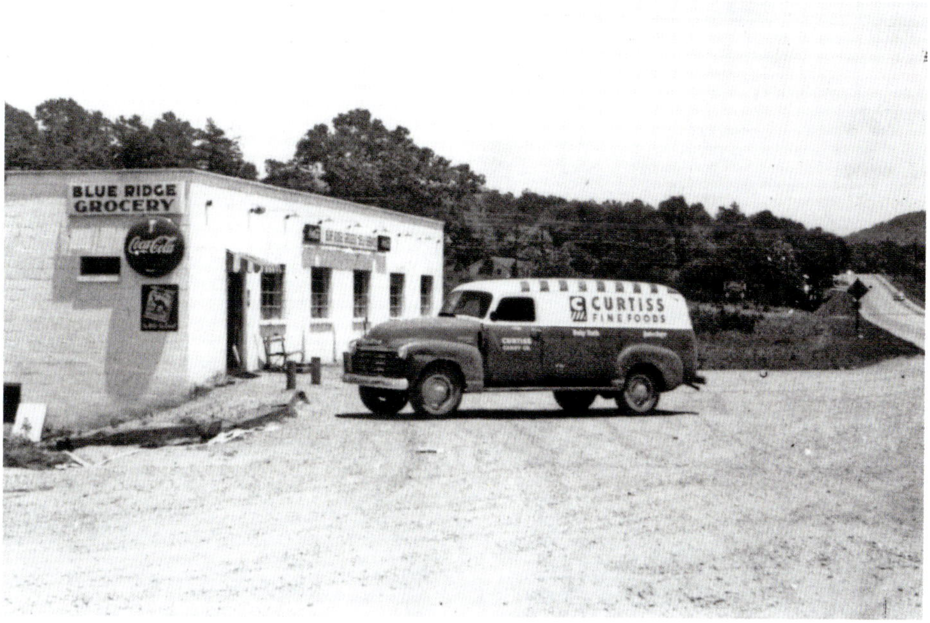

Blue Ridge Grocery, owned and operated by Willard Sterling Browning from 1946 to 1966, was near the intersection of Highway 70 and Blue Ridge Road. Browning began with a small open-air vegetable and fruit stand. In the 1950s, he built a larger masonry building with living quarters in the rear. The self-service grocery carried meat, produce, and a full grocery line. The building still stands but is currently vacant.

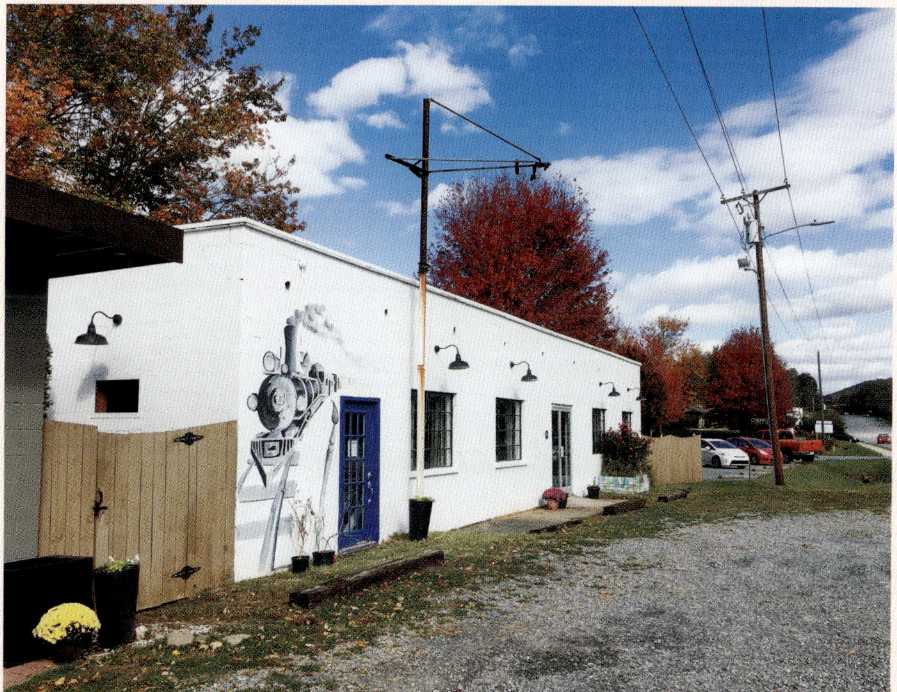

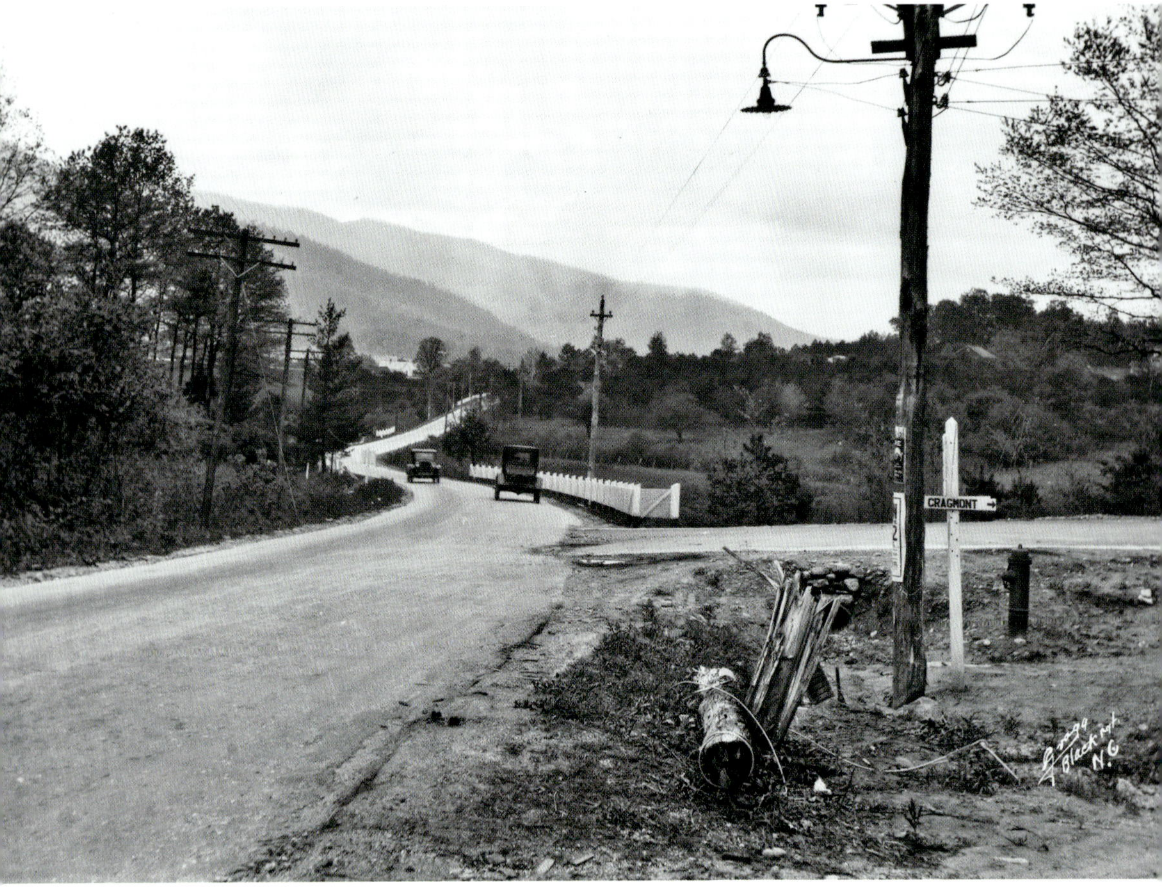

Downtown has grown significantly in the last 75 years, as can been seen by comparing the Gragg photograph above looking west toward the intersection of State Street and Cragmont Road with a modern-day photograph taken at the same location. The road has been widened from two lanes to five. A sidewalk and traffic lights have been installed. Businesses have been built and rebuilt on either side of the road. The mountains in the distance, however, remain much the same.

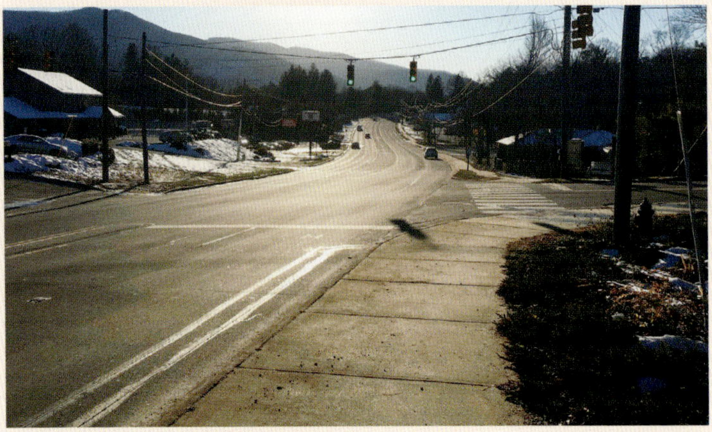

CHAPTER 4

Cool Mountain Air

Lodging, Sanatoriums, and Assemblies

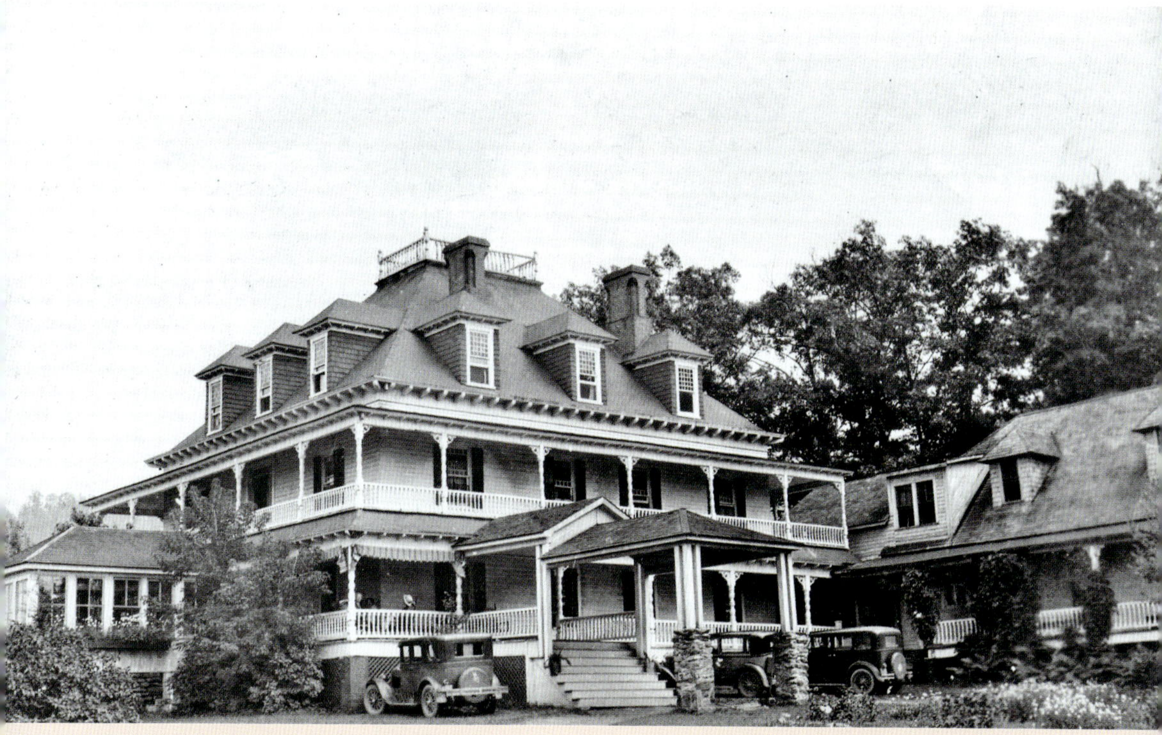

One of the earliest hotels in Black Mountain was the Mount Mitchell Hotel, which around 1885 abutted the railroad tracks on North Dougherty Street, the present location of Cove Auto Repair. The hotel was owned by Joseph Montraville "Mont" Stepp and his wife, Elizabeth Stepp Cordell, and was designed by notable architect George Capes Bonniwell. In 1890, the Stepps sold the hotel to Natt Atkinson, likely the same Atkinson who would become one of six shareholders in the newly formed Black Mountain Hotel Company in 1896. Throughout its life, the names Mount Mitchell Hotel and Black Mountain Hotel appear to have been used interchangeably. In January 1903, the hotel burned. Though no one perished, Gertrude Sprague, the manager, sustained severe burns to her face and neck.

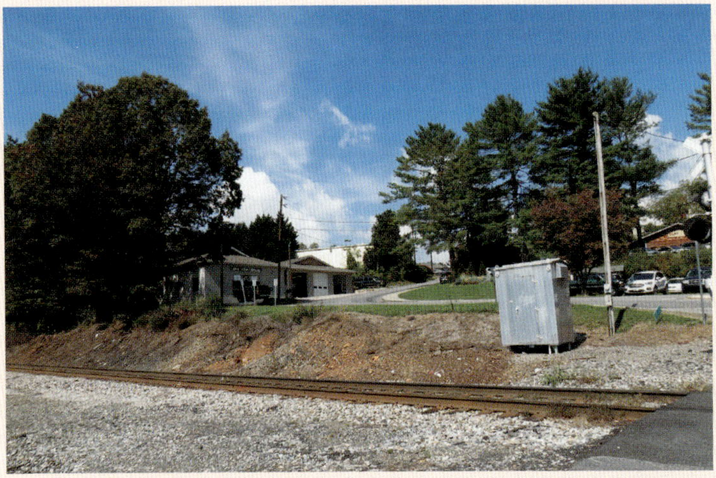

John A. Bell purchased the Mount Mitchell Hotel property in 1905. He finished erecting the Gladstone Hotel on the property in 1907. The hotel changed hands again in 1911 and 1913. In 1913, it was purchased by Emory L. Wilson and C. Gresham, and the name was changed to the Gresham Hotel. By the middle of 1916, Gresham transferred the hotel entirely to Wilson, who was managing it. In the early 1920s, the hotel's 40 rooms only operated for four months during the summer, and prices ranged from $1 to $3 a night. Locals remember its ballroom, which hosted dances and moving pictures. It closed in the 1930s and burned before 1942. When Cove Auto Repair expanded in 2016, it unearthed a layer of singed wood, glass, and nails undoubtedly from either the Gresham or the Black Mountain.

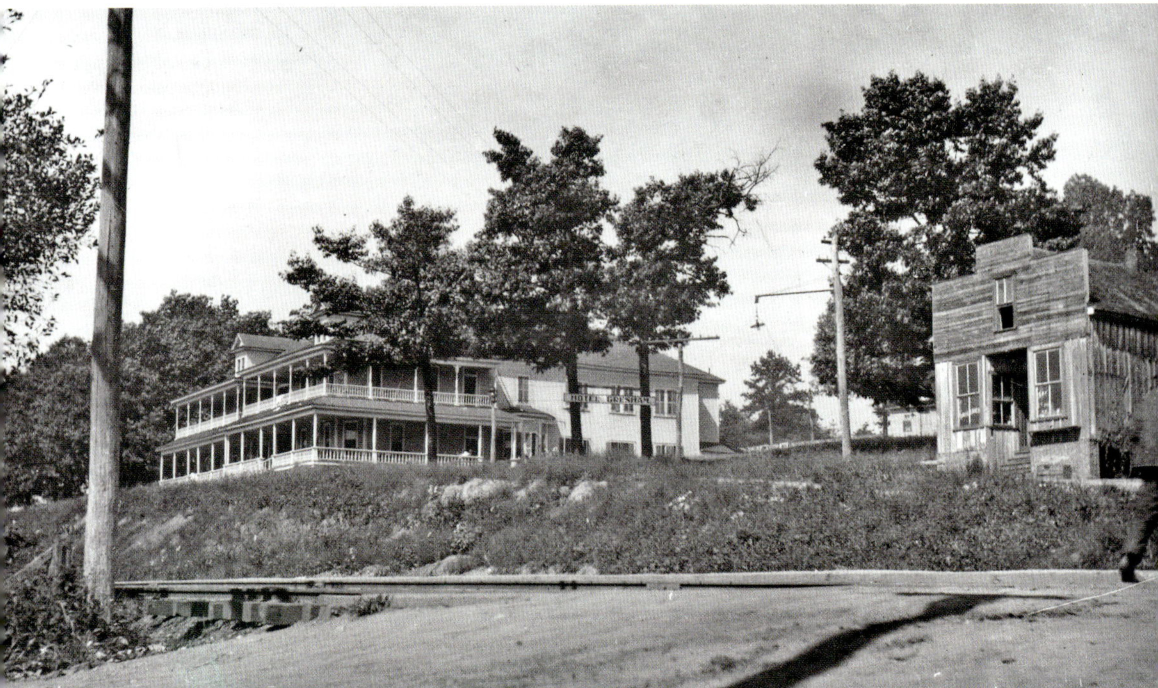

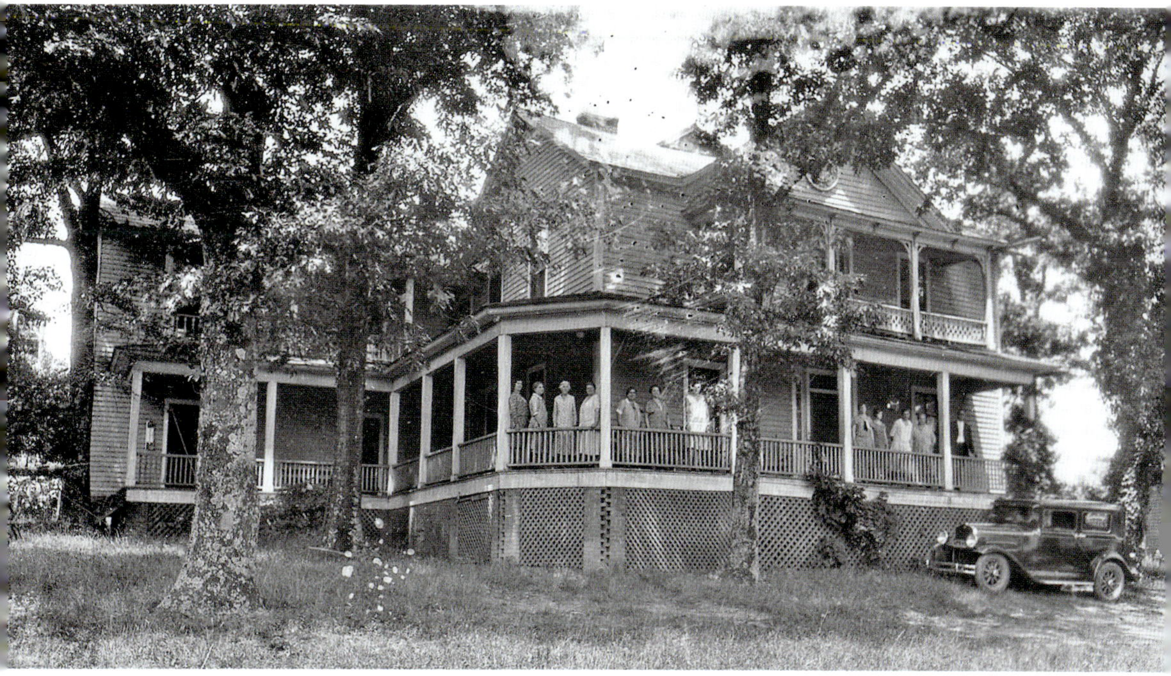

As more and more tourists descended upon the town, more hotels and boardinghouses opened. According to Black Mountain High School's 1932 History of Black Mountain, across from the present Monte Vista Hotel in an area now occupied by a car-wash, the Washington House was opened around 1894 by Julia and Louis Washington, a third cousin of George Washington. Julia died in 1895. The property changed hands a couple of times; in 1908, P.A. Cauble and his wife, Laura Ann Cauble, moved from Salisbury and purchased the home. Reports in the *Salisbury Evening Post* indicate that Cauble sold his grocery there to begin a mercantile in Black Mountain. Cauble died in 1912 of heart trouble. The following year, Laura Cauble transferred part of the property to her daughter Jennie L. Shuman, and by 1915, the pair were operating the Cauble House, a 25-room hotel that also served meals.

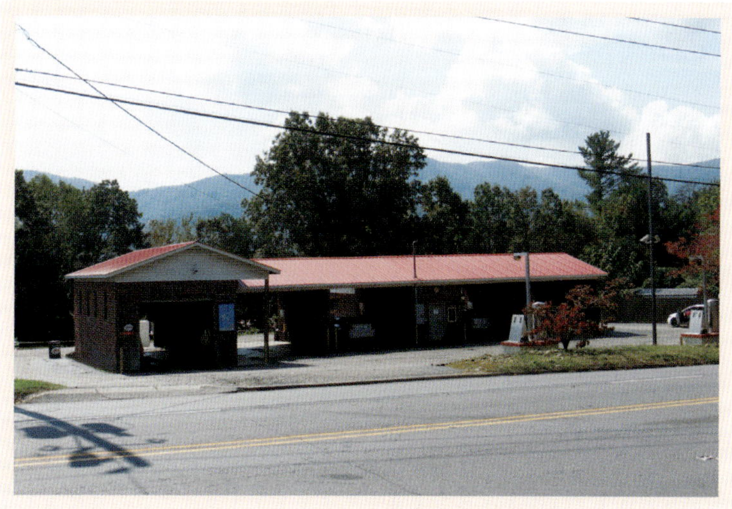

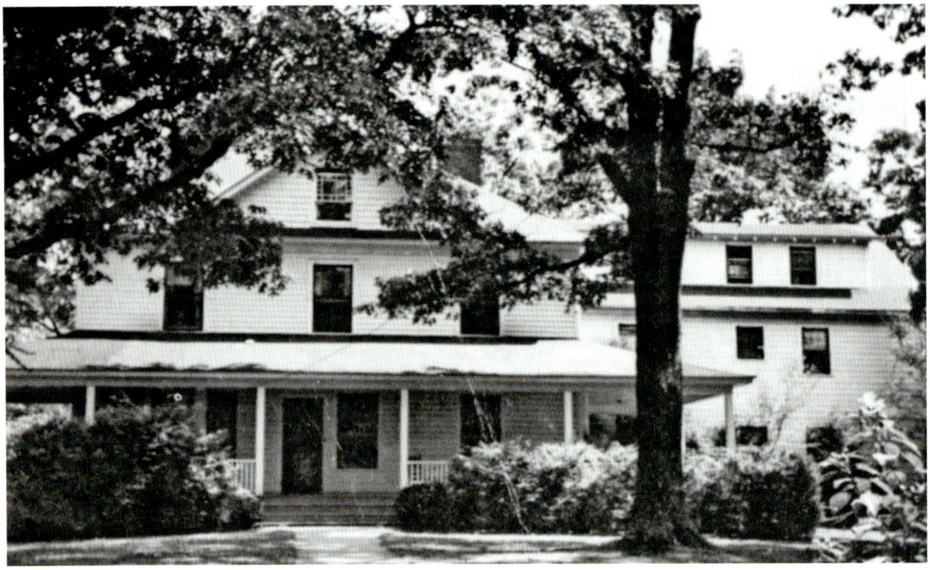

Originally known as Mountain View, the home pictured here—the first built in the Dougherty Heights Historic District—was constructed in 1897 by Silas and Martha Dougherty as a residence. When their sons left home, the Doughertys and their daughter Sadie began to rent rooms to boarders. In the early 1900s, Sadie and her husband, Alfred Forbes Tyson Sr., took over operations and began calling the residence Dougherty Heights Inn. Around 1940, they enlarged the inn, adding a wing of guestrooms for a total of 22 bedrooms and seven baths. They operated the inn until 1960. Upon Sadie's death in 1970, the inn was sold, and though it operated as Dougherty Heights for several years, it was renamed the Red Rocker Inn in 1973, which it is still known as today.

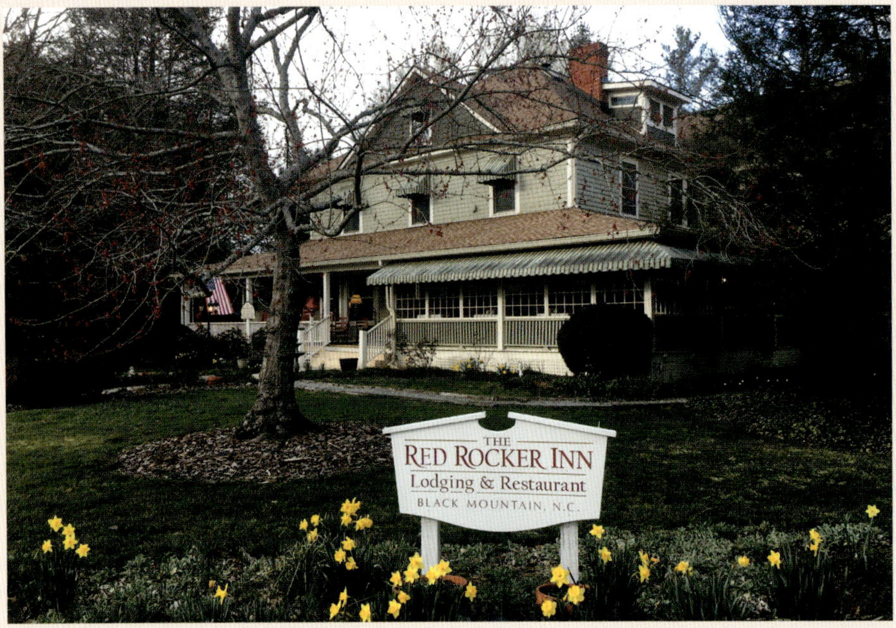

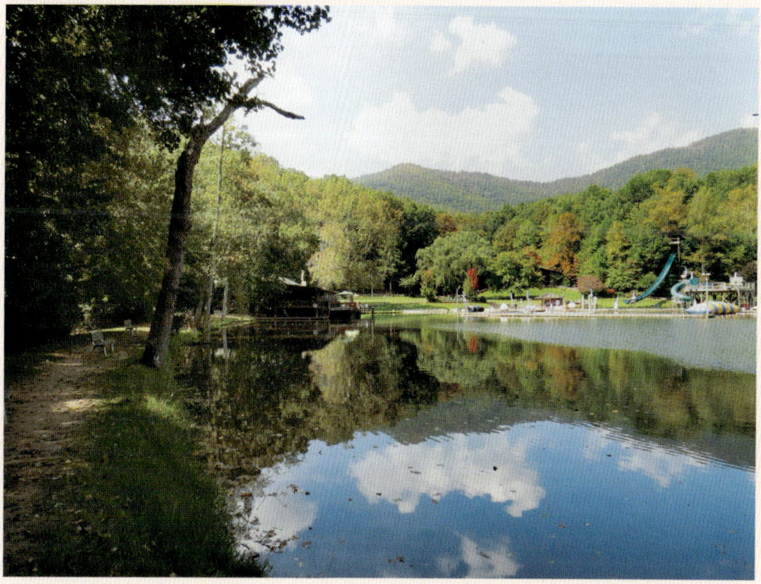

Opened in 1925 by Edwin Wiley Grove, who most notably constructed the Grove Park Inn, Lake Eden and its surrounding structures, pictured here, were built as a summer resort. The first summer, the resort operated as a dance hall and restaurant but was not a financial success. The following summer, Grove used the property as a girls' camp, Lake Eden Camp, and artists' colony, the Camp of Scholar Gypsies. In 1927, the lake was leased for use as Lake Eden Inn. Black Mountain College purchased the property in 1937. It took several years for the students and faculty to winterize the buildings and construct new buildings in order to move in, and during the interim, college faculty, staff, and students operated the Lake Eden Inn. From 1941 until 1957, the college operated year-round at Lake Eden. Since 1956, the Lake Eden property has been home to Camp Rockmont for Boys during the summer.

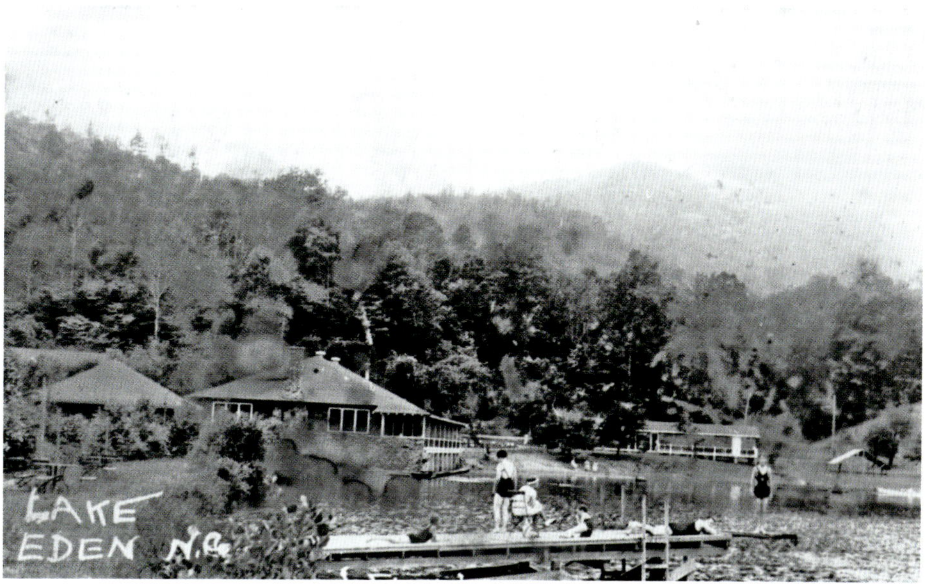

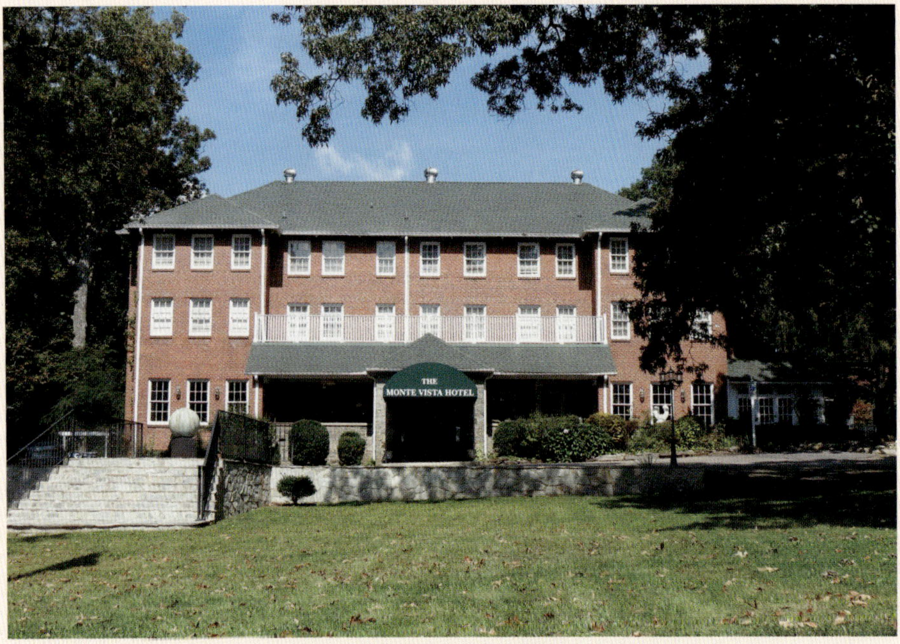

In December 1919, Lucien Emmett and Rosalie Jumper Phillips finalized the purchase of the old Kerlee School. The following year, the couple began operating the Monte Vista Hotel, pictured here, out of the wood-frame building that boasted steam heat, private baths, and no sick guests accepted. In 1936, they built a new three-story building just to the west of the hotel. The new Monte Vista Manor opened to guests on Thursday, August 5, 1937. The new building, which still stands and operates as the Monte Vista Hotel today, had 30 guestrooms and 28 baths on the second and third floors, a large lobby and dining room on the first floor, and a recreation room with a billiard table in the basement. The wooden building was eventually torn down.

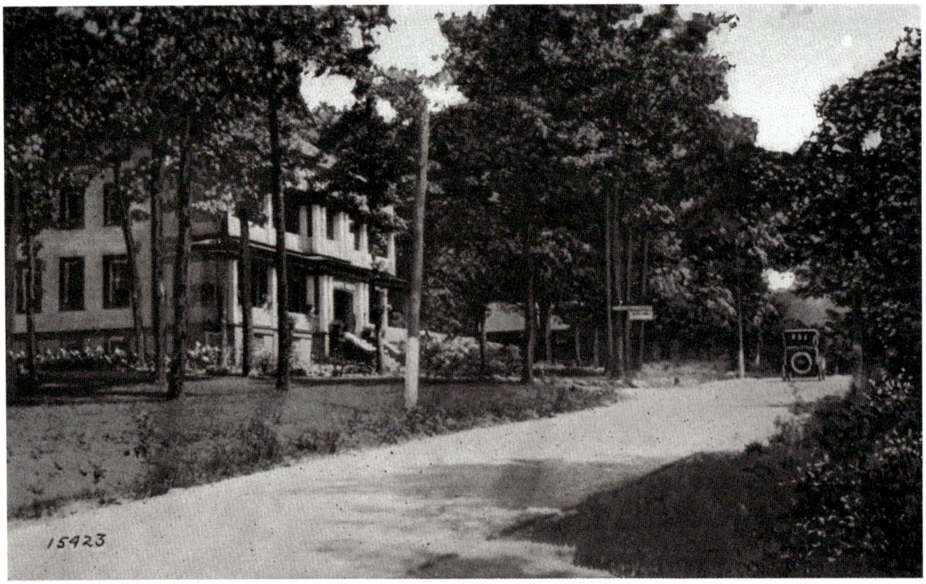

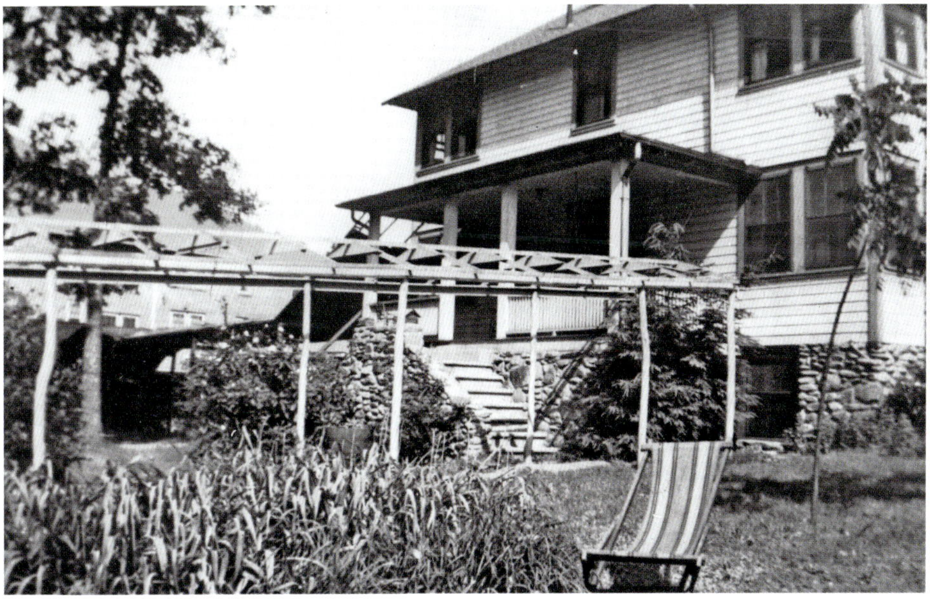

A year prior to erecting the brick building, the Phillipses built a two-story frame annex to the Monte Vista Hotel, pictured here, with a small lobby, 15 guestrooms, and eight bathrooms. Along with a nearby two-story brick apartment building called the Monte Vista Apartments, the Phillipses supplied 90 guestrooms during the summer months. They also ran a small farm, which provided the hotel with vegetables, dairy, and special meat products.

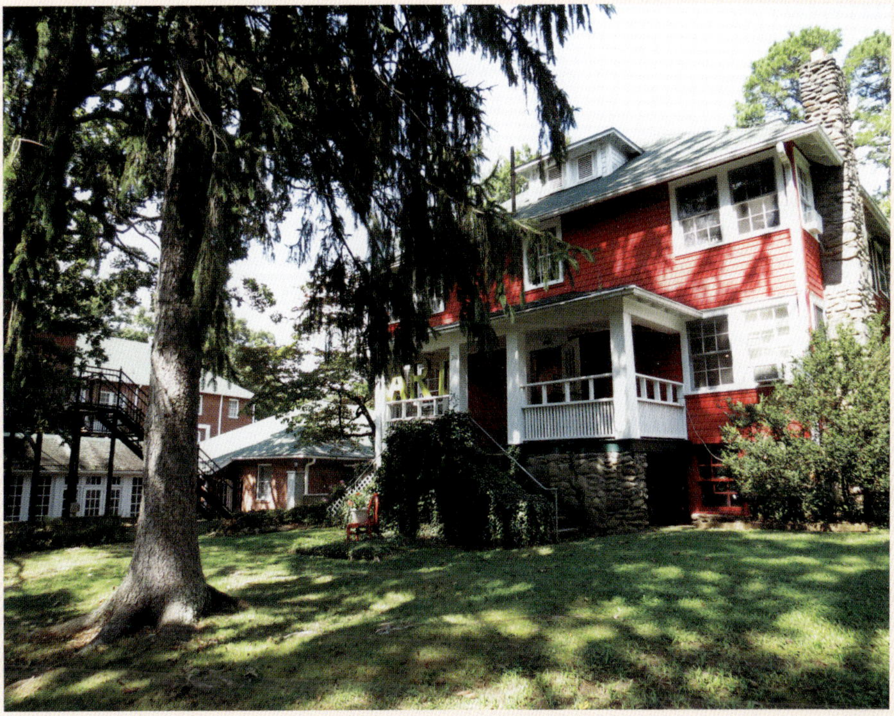

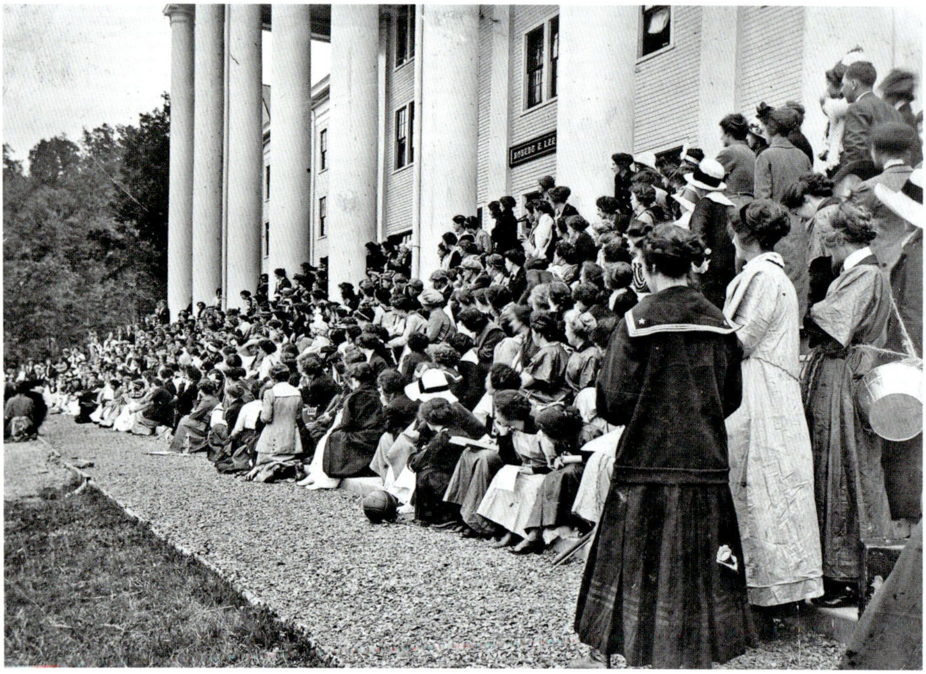

The photograph above, donated by Ann Ratcliffe, shows a YMCA Student Conference in 1915 on the steps of Robert E. Lee Hall at the YMCA Blue Ridge Association grounds. One of many Christian assemblies around Black Mountain, including Christmount, Ridgecrest, Cragmont, and Montreat, Blue Ridge Assembly, as it is now known, was founded in 1906 by Willis D. Weatherford. The name of Lee Hall was changed in 2015 to Eureka Hall to commemorate the date in 1906 when Weatherford climbed a tree and surveyed the potential grounds for his assembly. At the top, he declared, "Eureka, we have found it!" The building was erected in 1912 just to the northwest of the famous tree.

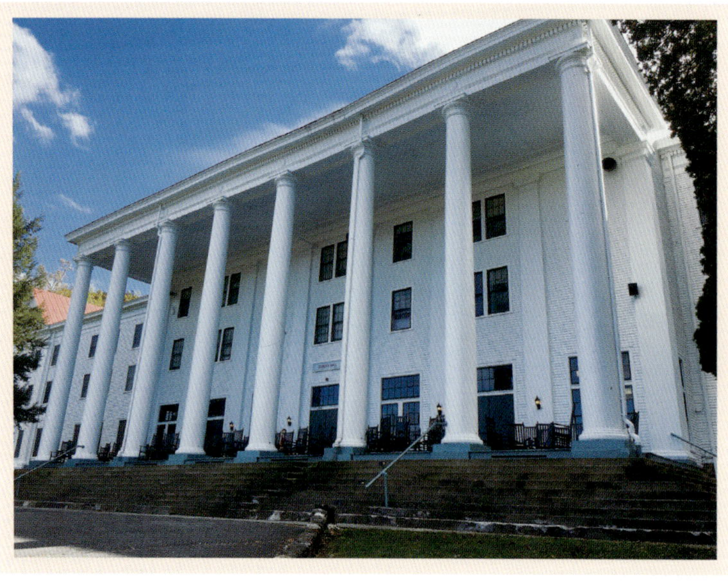

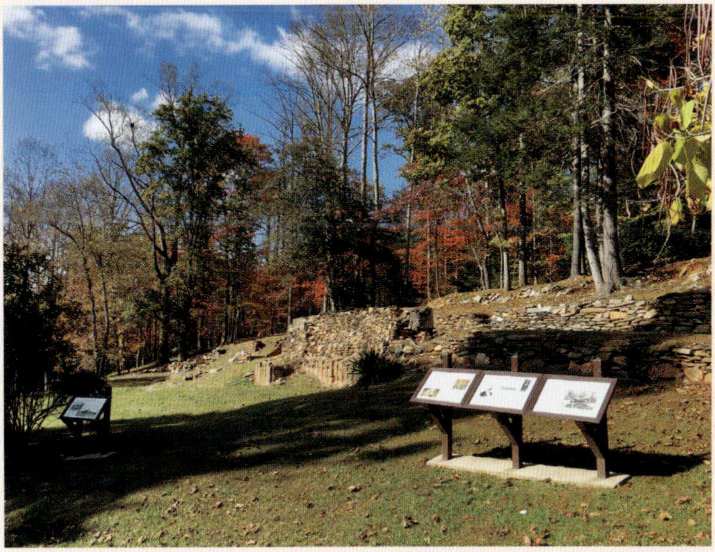

Rafael Guastavino, an emigrant from Spain who constructed tiled domes across the country with his son, came to the area in 1894 to work on the famed Biltmore Estate and decided to stay. Though he was known for his fireproof tile work, his rambling retirement home was wooden. The estate, which he called Rhododendron but locals knew as "the Spanish Castle," would eventually contain a gatehouse, wine cellar, kiln, pond, and farm. Guastavino died in 1908 at his Black Mountain home, where his wife, Francisca, continued to reside reclusively until she was badly burned in a fire around 1943. After she died on January 28, 1946, in a nursing home, the estate was sold to the Disciples of Christ to build Christmount Christian Conference Center, and the dilapidated house was eventually razed. The wine cellar and a kiln still stand.

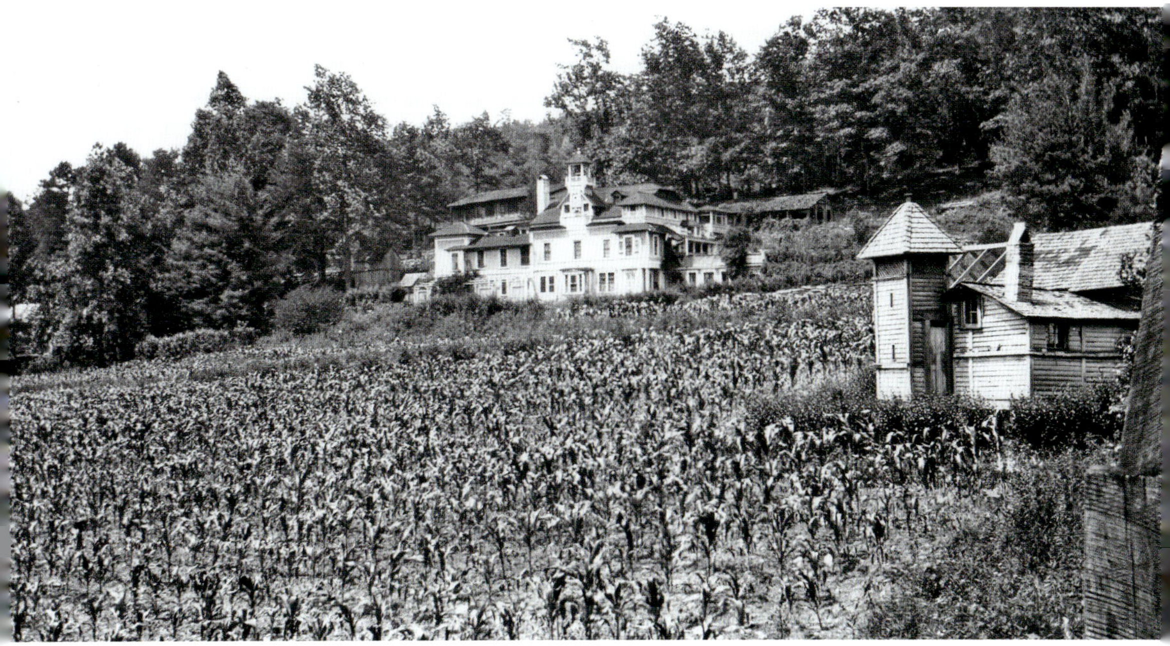

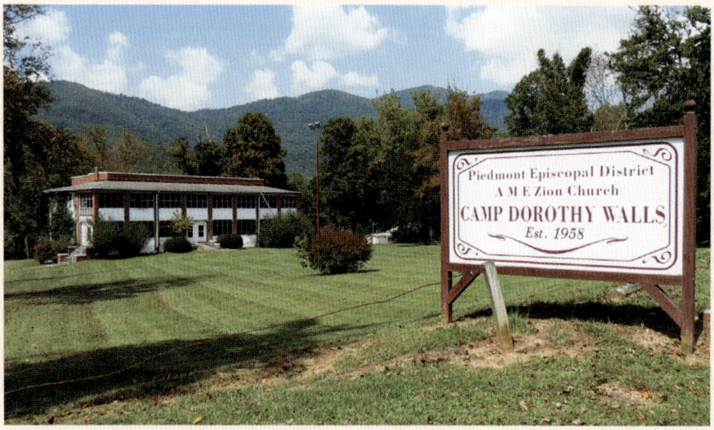

People also came for their health, and many sanatoriums treated tuberculosis and other pulmonary illnesses. In 1904, Dr. Isaac James Archer began work on a three-story building for the Fellowship Association of the Royal League of Chicago. By September 1905, a large and modern sanatorium opened primarily to serve members of the league. Three months later, the sanatorium was at capacity, and the league erected eight additional cottages on the site. In February 1920, the sanatorium burned, and the main building and cottages were replaced with a brick-framed building with screened porches that still stands. It was sold to the AME Zion Church for Camp Dorothy Walls in 1958.

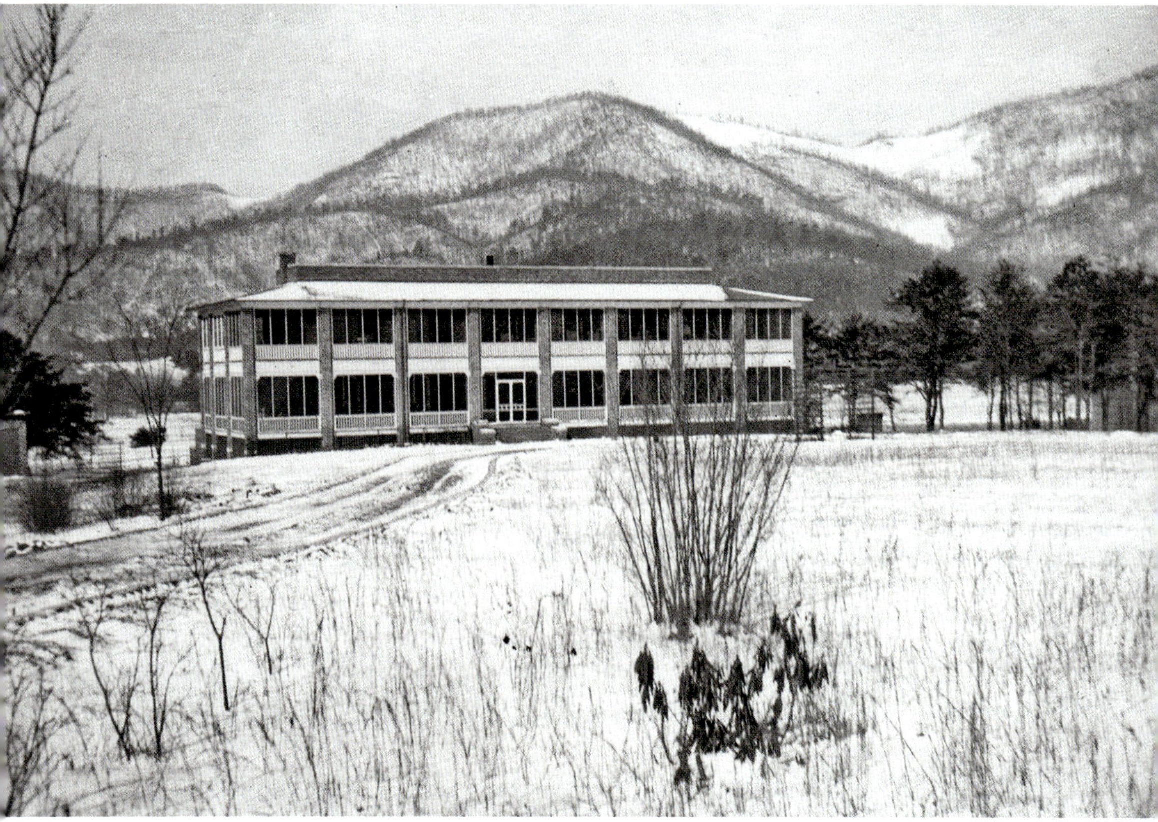

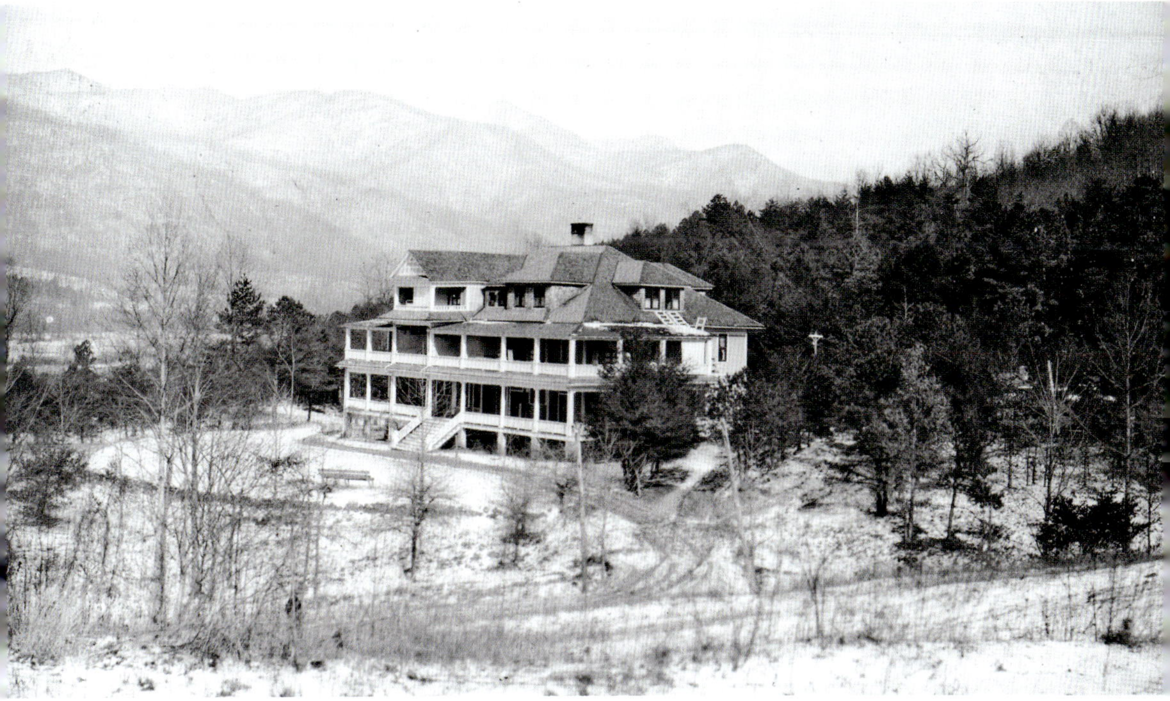

In 1905, the Harrison Mountain Air Sanatorium was incorporated by Dr. Archer and others just north of the Royal League on the opposite site of North Fork Road, in the present location of Cragmont Assembly. In 1916, the company officially changed its name to the Cragmont Sanatorium, though it had used the name since at least 1908, and operated with Dr. Archer as director and head doctor. The company ceased operations around 1940 and officially dissolved in 1945, the same year Archer died, and the land was sold to the assembly. The building pictured above was demolished and a new building erected on the same site in 1979 for use as the assembly's conference center.

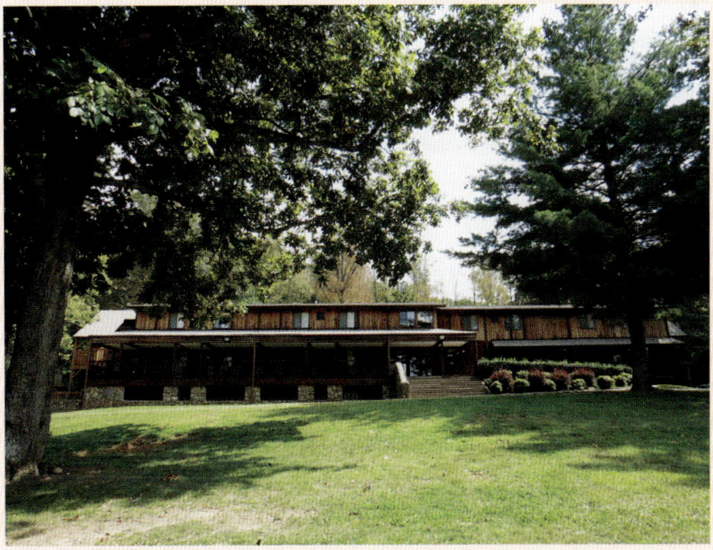

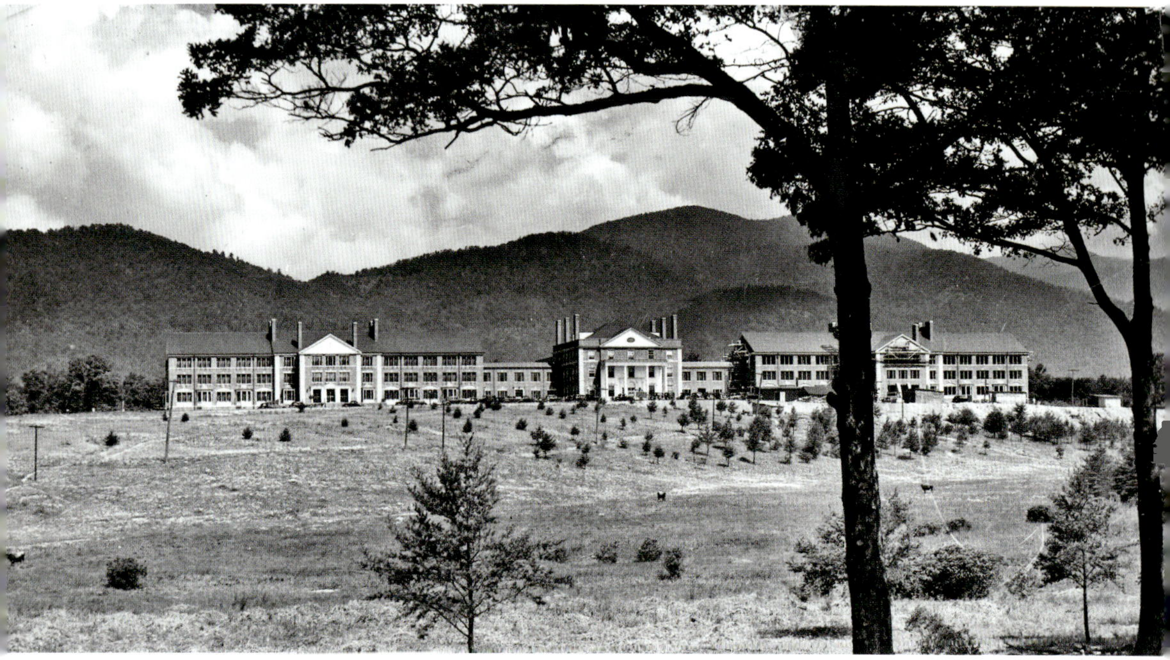

When the Western North Carolina Sanatorium, operated by the state, opened in 1937, there was already a long waiting list and plans to enlarge. The main building contained storage space, a bakery, an autopsy room, a dining room and kitchen, office space, laboratories, x-rays, exam rooms, dental offices, a large operating pavilion, and a 500-seat auditorium with a grand piano and movie projector. Each patient room had a sleeping porch. In the c. 1952 Edward DuPuy photograph above, the eastern wing—for African American patients—is under construction. Medical developments decreased the number of TB patients, and in the 1970s, the facility began expanding its services. It is now known as the Black Mountain Neuro-Medical Treatment Center.

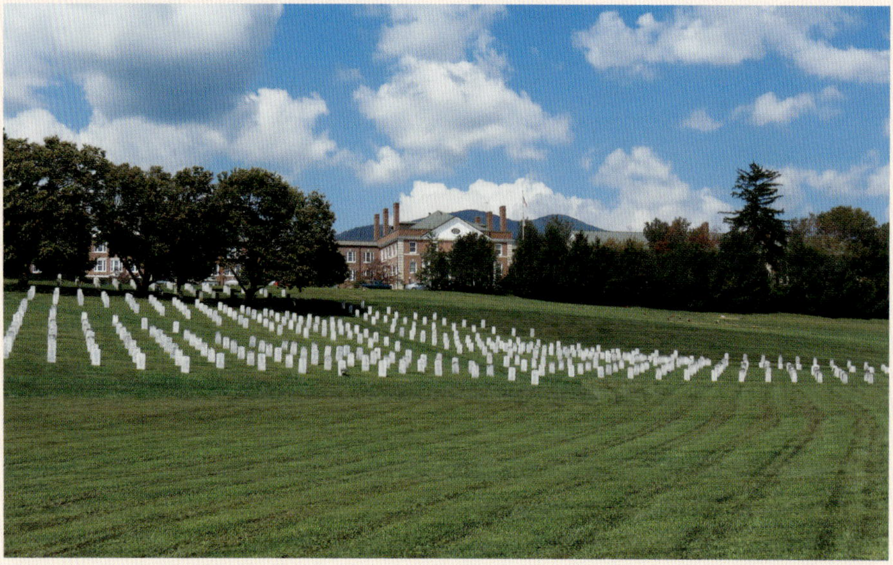

CHAPTER 5

THE GOOD OLD DAYS

WORSHIP AND EDUCATION

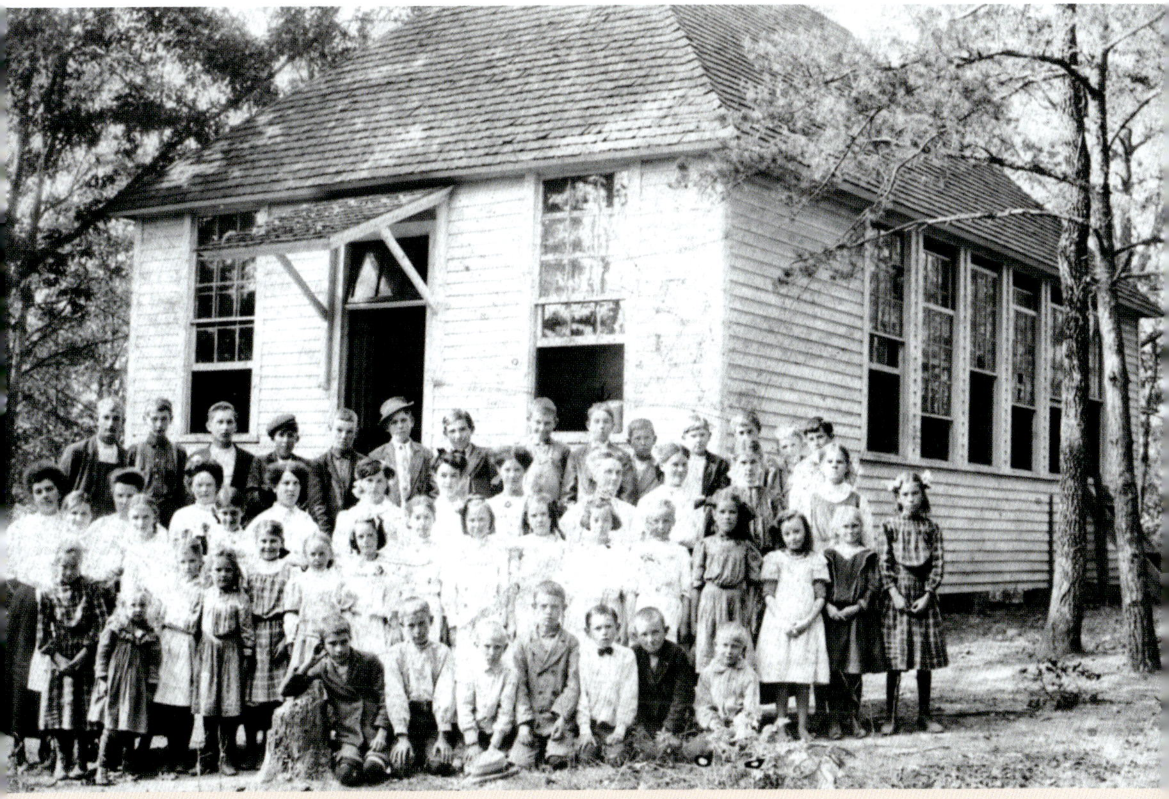

Until 1919, most students studied in one-room schoolhouses such as Tabernacle, Oak Grove, Kerlee, Flat Creek, Parker Hill, North Fork, and Lance, with one teacher in charge of multiple grades. The Lance School, pictured here, was near the intersection of Old US 70 and North Fork Road, according to Robert Goodson. In 1919, the new Black Mountain School was constructed to accommodate all the children in the Black Mountain, Ridgecrest, and Lance School Districts. Though Ridgecrest was in favor of consolidation, Lance was against it, and the consolidation failed. In 1921, Lance considered joining the Swannanoa Consolidated District, but finally, at the end of the 1921 term, it decided to consolidate into the Black Mountain District, and Lance School closed.

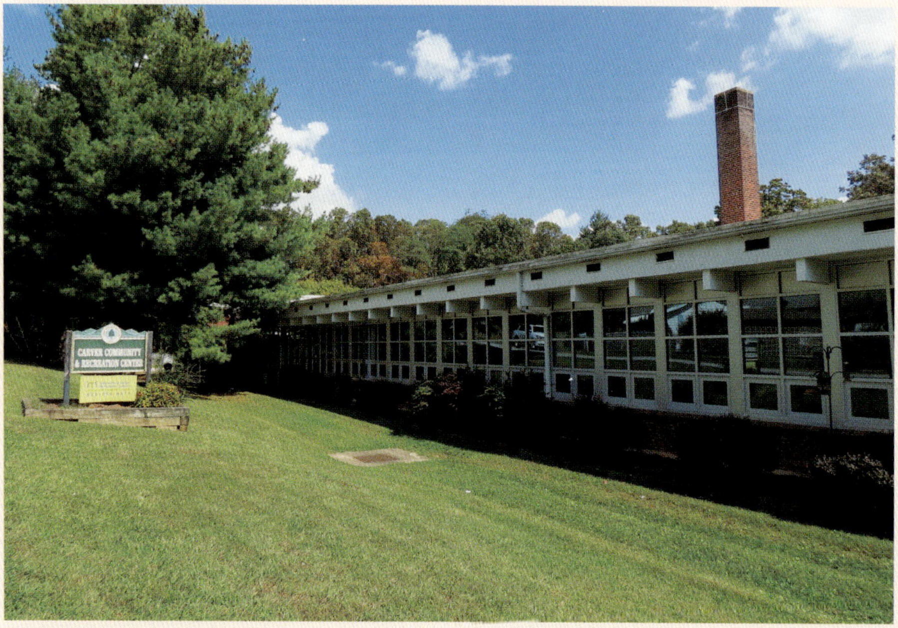

As early as 1886, the Flat Creek Road School in the Brookside community served black students, who were also taught in the log two-room Clearview Elementary. In 1942, the building was replaced by the stone structure seen below. In 1951, the school board began construction on a modern brick building to replace the aging stone structure. On September 2, 1952, George Washington Carver Elementary opened in the new brick building, serving 140 students. Carver closed in 1966 with school desegregation. It is now the Carver Community Center, owned by the Town of Black Mountain.

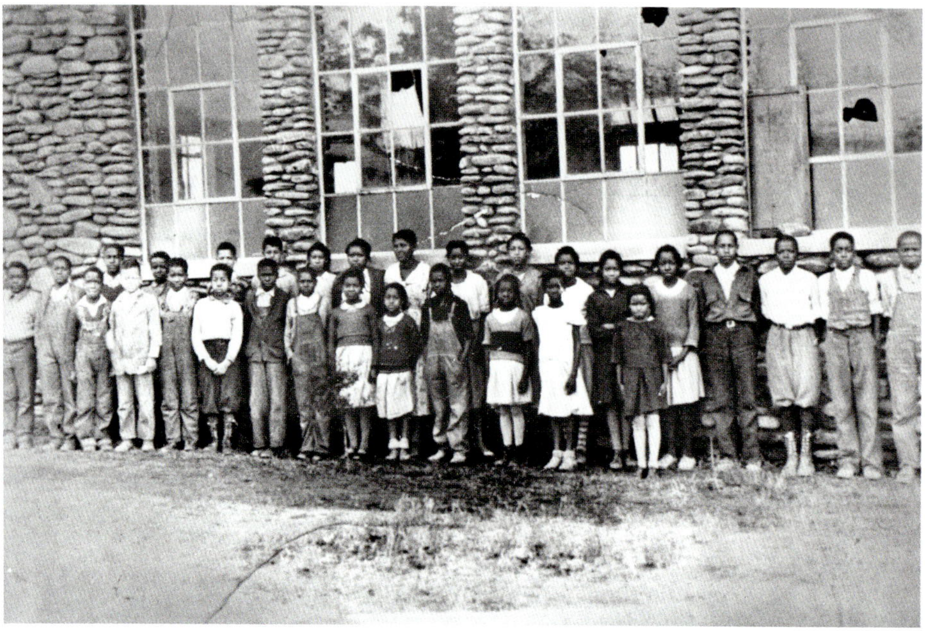

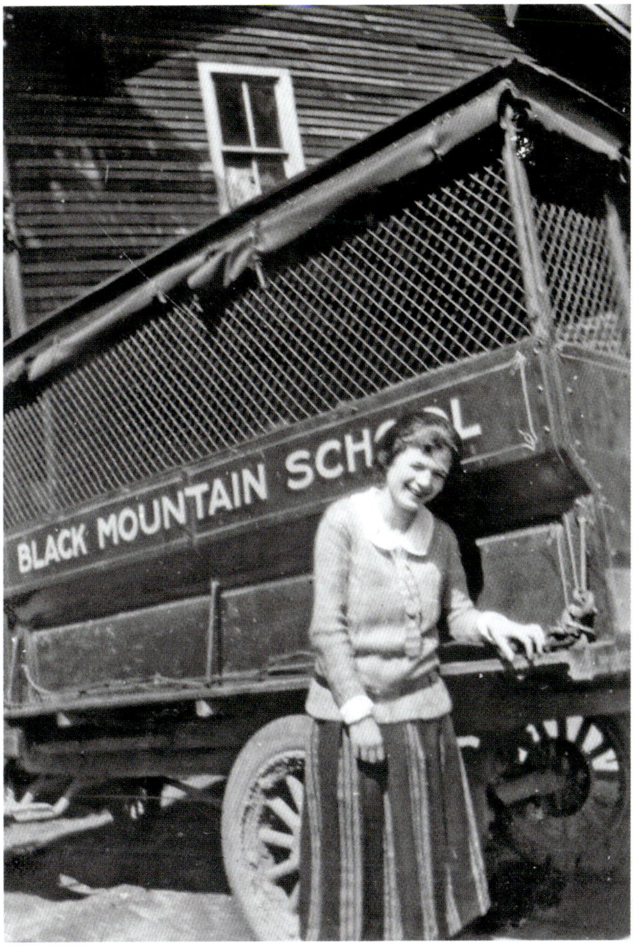

Black Mountain School was in operation prior to the turn of the 20th century. The school, which served nine grades, constructed a new building in 1910 and an 800-person auditorium in 1913. In 1917, a new building was under construction on State Street; it served primary through high school starting around 1919. At left, Alice Craven Mohr stands in front of her school bus. Part of the reasoning behind consolidating schools, beyond providing better facilities and more teachers, was that a consolidated school could be operated at less cost, even when factoring in having to bus children who were accustomed to walking to small schools near their homes.

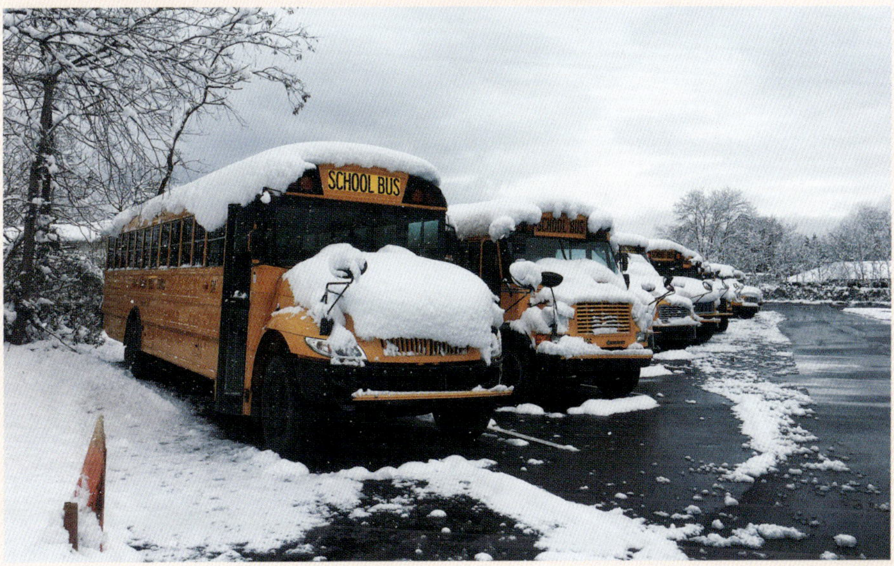

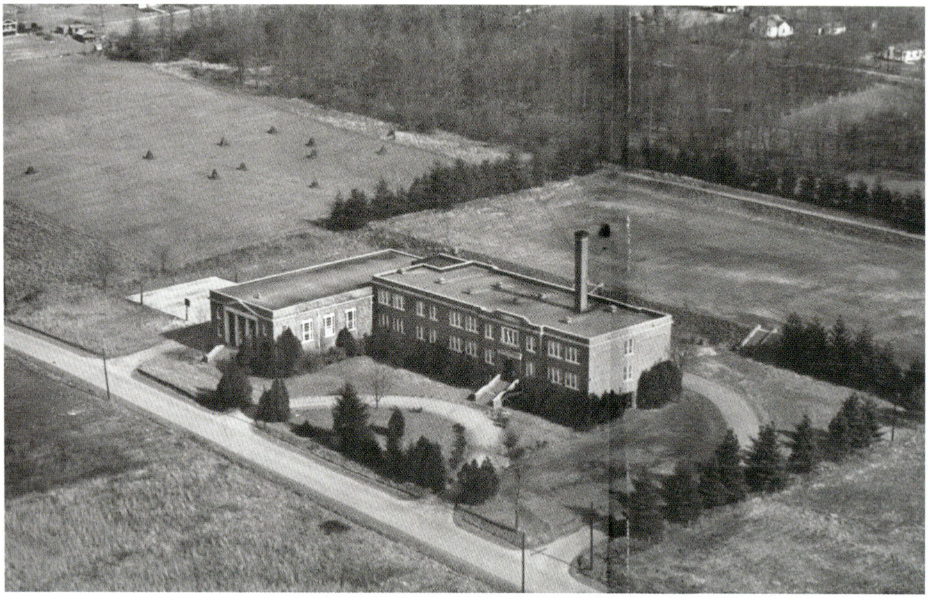

In July 1926, the board of education purchased property on Flat Creek Road for Black Mountain High School. In December 1927, the new modernly equipped high school, pictured above in 1951, was dedicated. The school had a domestic service department, lunch room, and gymnasium. When the high school vacated this building in 1955 during consolidation, Black Mountain Grammar School (grades five through eight) moved in. In 1991, the middle grades moved to the old Owen High School on Old US 70, and the site became Black Mountain Elementary School. Only the original gymnasium still stands.

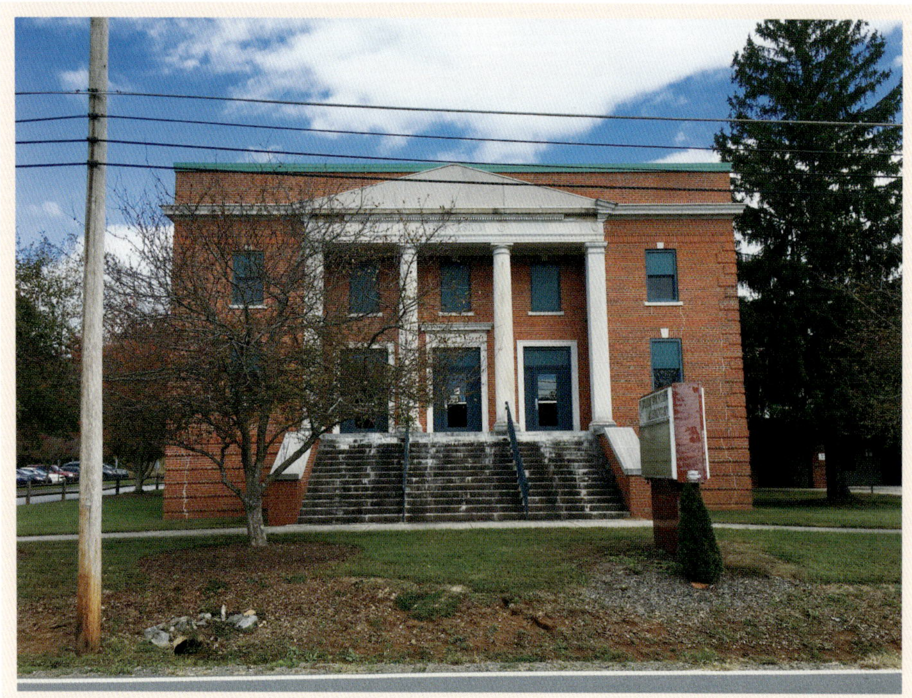

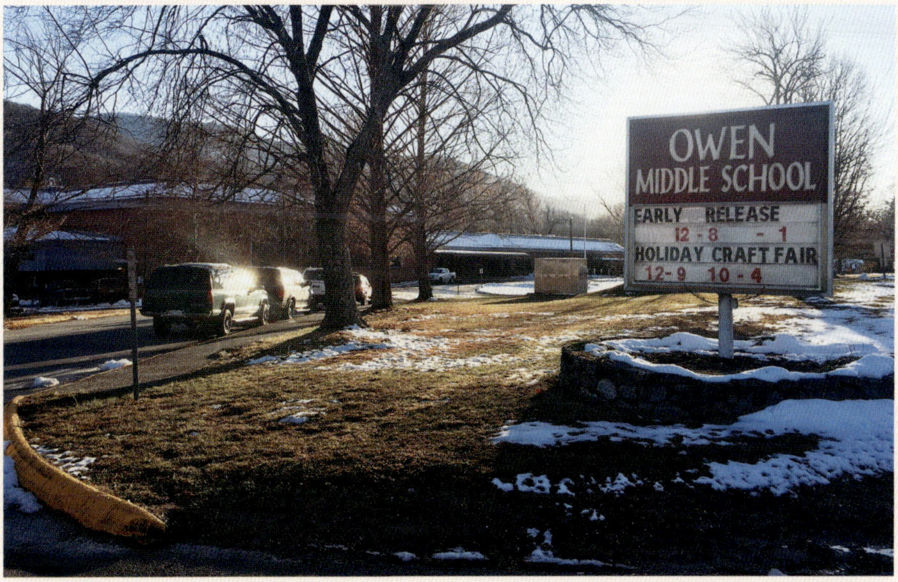

In 1955, Black Mountain and Swannanoa High Schools consolidated grades nine through 12 into Charles D. Owen High School. In the 1960 photograph below, from left to right, Patsy Lee, Gail Hall, and Brenda Lindsey make up the first row of majorettes, and Rita Putnam, Linda Connor, and Judy Raines stand in the back. There was never a high school in the valley for African American students. Instead, they were bussed to Stephens Lee High School in Asheville. In 1964, those in favor of desegregation cited that every day, 78 to 85 black students were bussed past Owen High School on their way into Asheville. This building became Owen Middle School on Old US 70 in 1991, when the new Owen High School on Lake Eden Road opened.

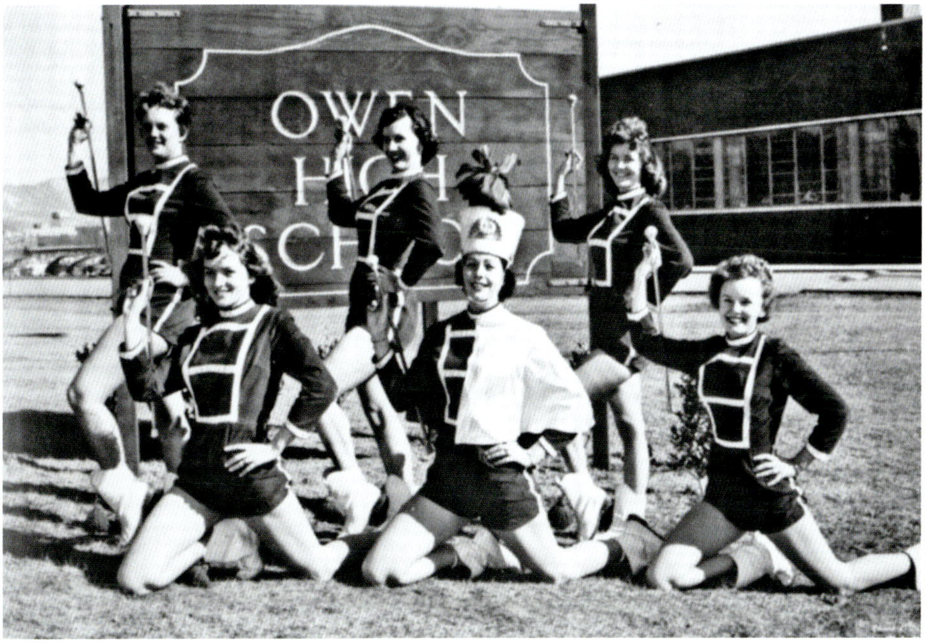

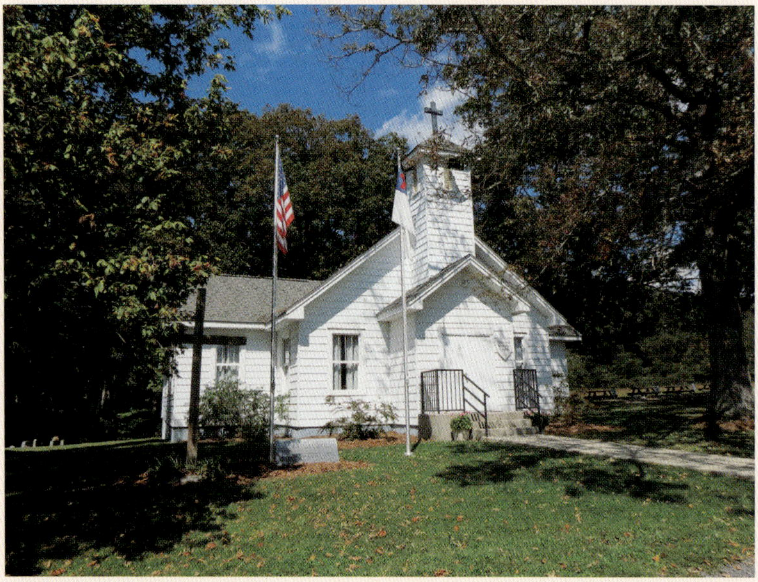

According to Robert Goodson, Tabernacle Meeting House was used as a church and a schoolhouse and was established by at least 1837, the first church building constructed in the community. By March 1848, there were 46 members of the church, including two enslaved people, Rose and Coleman. The log building, chinked with red clay mud, had windows covered by shutters attached with leather. Women sat on one side of the church and men on the other. The school operated until around 1880. A new church building, pictured below around 1917, was erected in 1887, but due to its height, it would sway in the wind. Considered unsafe, was torn down and rebuilt in 1927. The rebuilt structure still stands today.

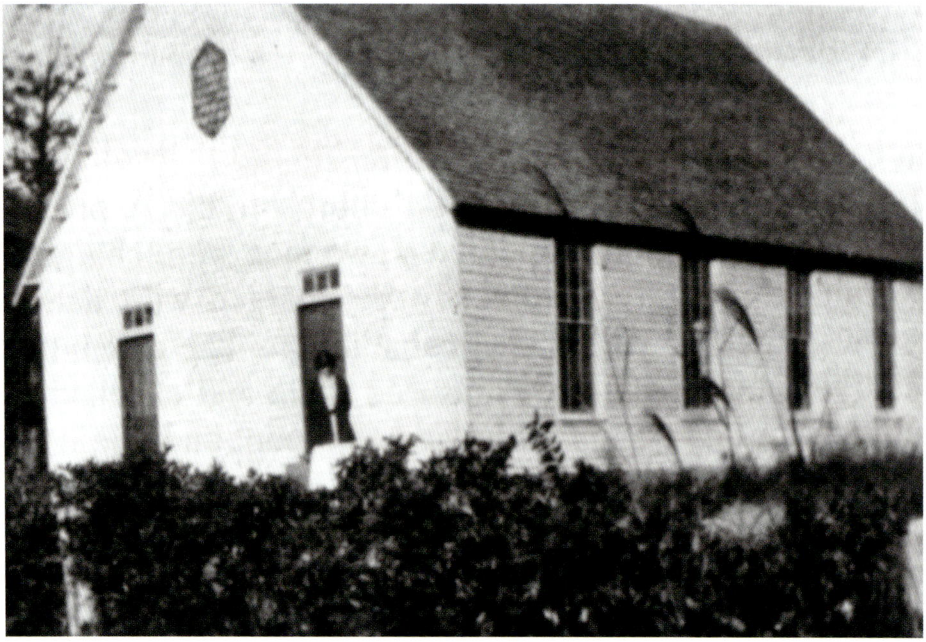

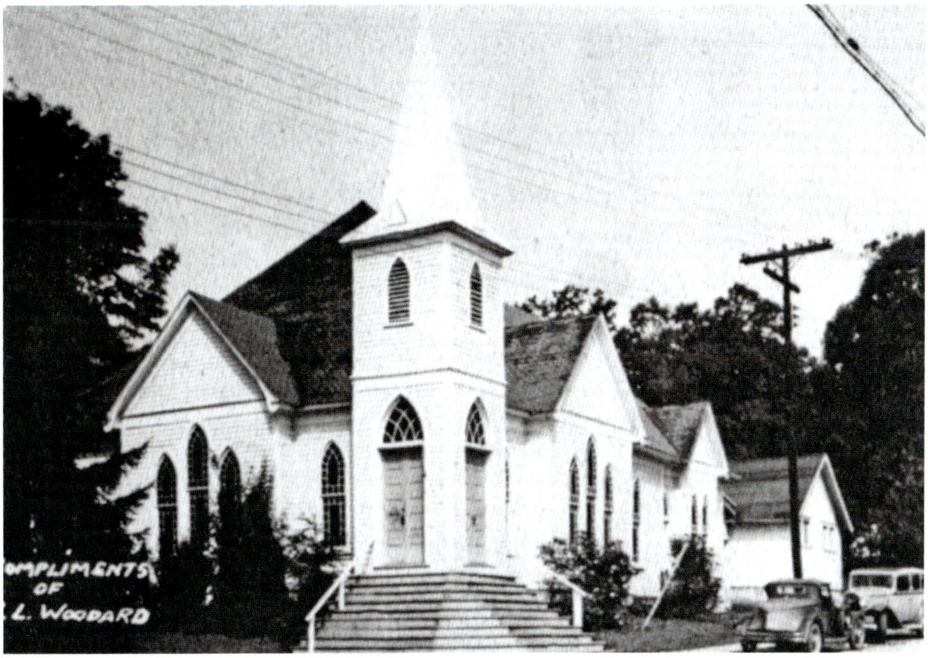

When Black Mountain Methodist Church was founded around 1890 out of Tabernacle, it met in the original Kerlee School House on the northeast corner of Montreat Road and State Street. The same year, the congregation built a church on what is now Church Street, not far from where the present building is now located. In 1912, the church acquired its present lot, built a new structure (seen around the 1930s above), tore down the old building, and used the lumber to build a parsonage. In 1938, a new brick parsonage that still stands was ready for occupancy. The old parsonage became a home to the church custodians but was torn down to make room for the new education building in 1954. The present brick building opened in 1962.

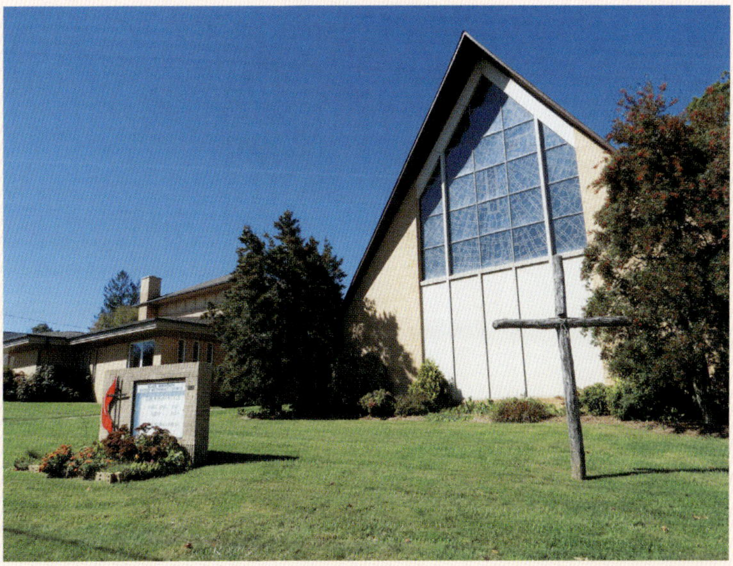

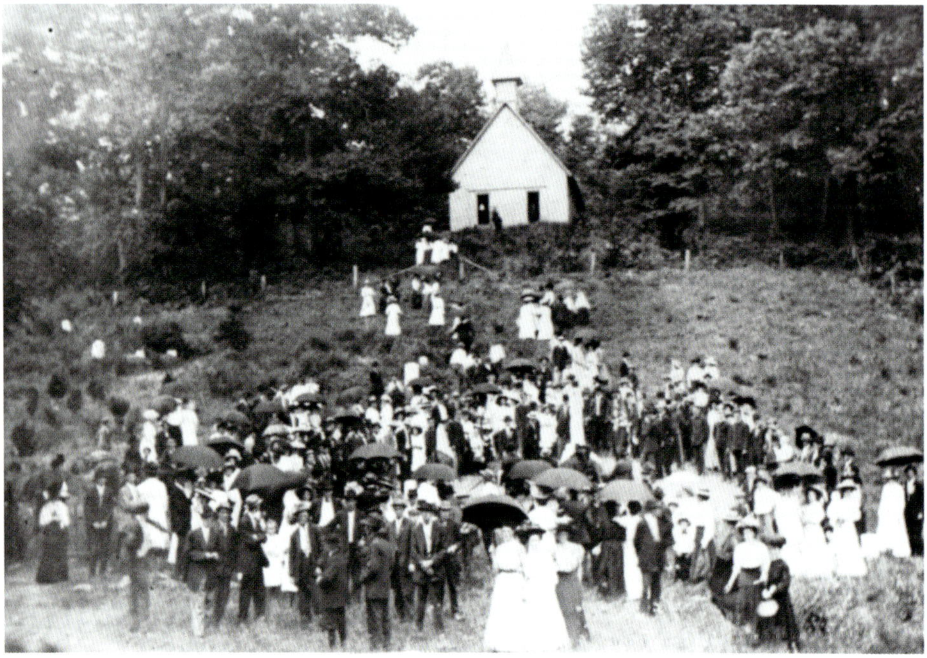

Prior to 1828, residents of the North Fork community founded a church. At that time, the parishioners met in Eldridge Burnett's home. In 1858, Eldridge's brother, Frederick, deeded the land for the first United Baptist Church of Christ at North Fork. In 1898, a new building, pictured above, was erected closer to town, and the name was changed to Mountain View Baptist Church. The church burned in February 1941, and a new rock-faced structure was built. In 1951, the City of Asheville rebuilt the church in its present location, as it needed the land the church and its graveyard sat on for the dam for a new reservoir. In 1952, before the valley was flooded, 260 graves were moved to the site of the new church.

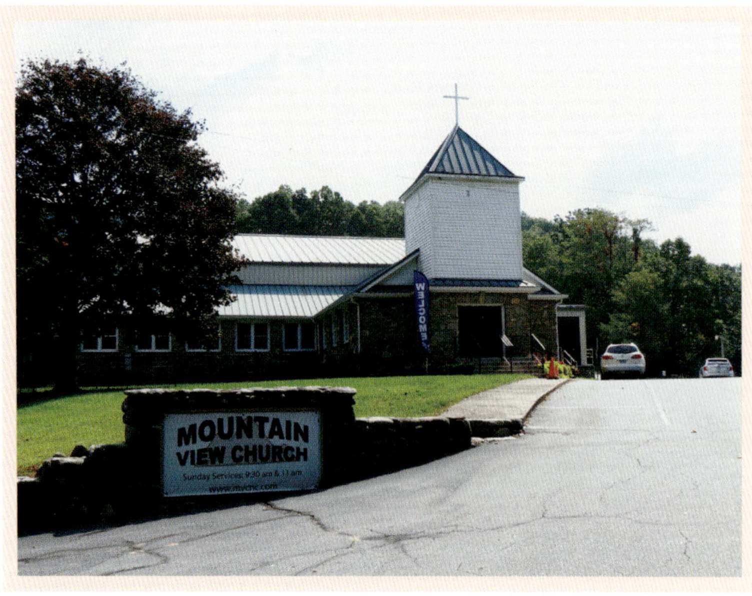

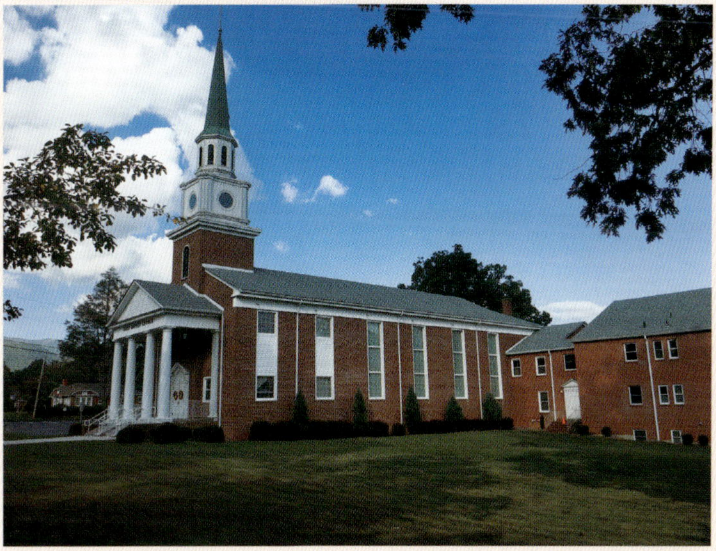

Black Mountain Baptist Church, now First Baptist, organized in 1905 in the former Kerlee School House. Two years later, the congregation purchased land fronting Montreat Road, and the first building was constructed (pictured below). In 1924, the first parsonage was built, seen to the right of the sanctuary. In 1933, the parsonage was converted to an education building and a new parsonage was built. In 1949, a new sanctuary replacing the 1907 building was completed. The church expanded again in 1957 with a new education building. In 1968, a new parsonage was built on Pine Street, and the old parsonage was converted to a nursery.

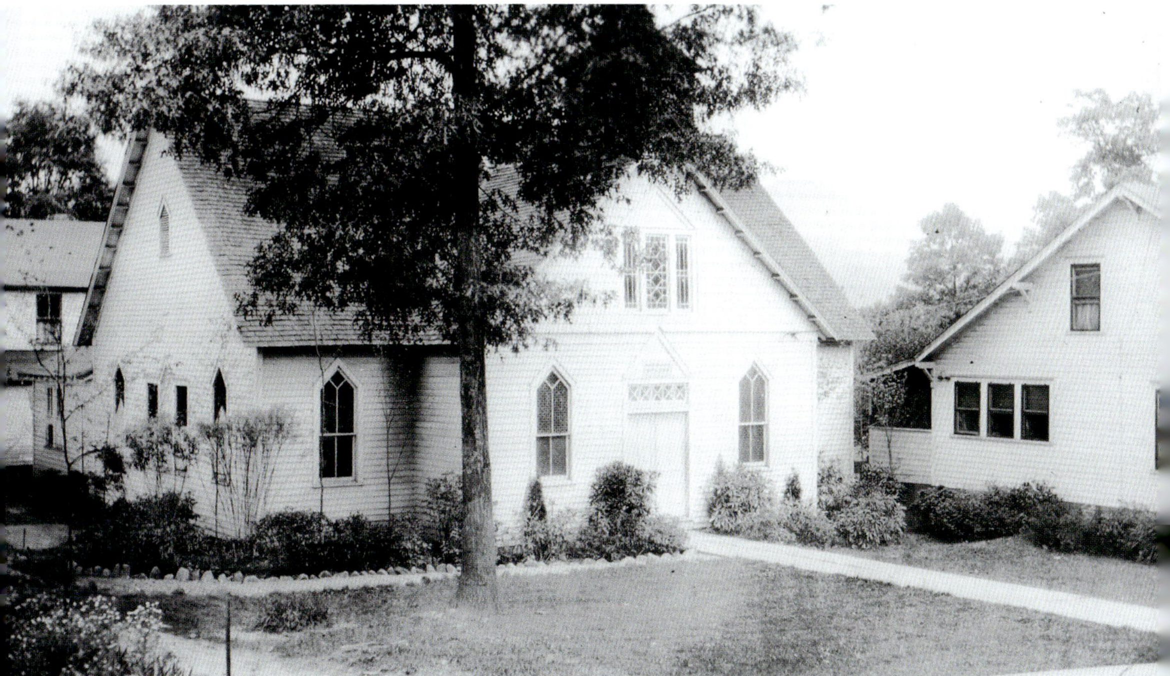

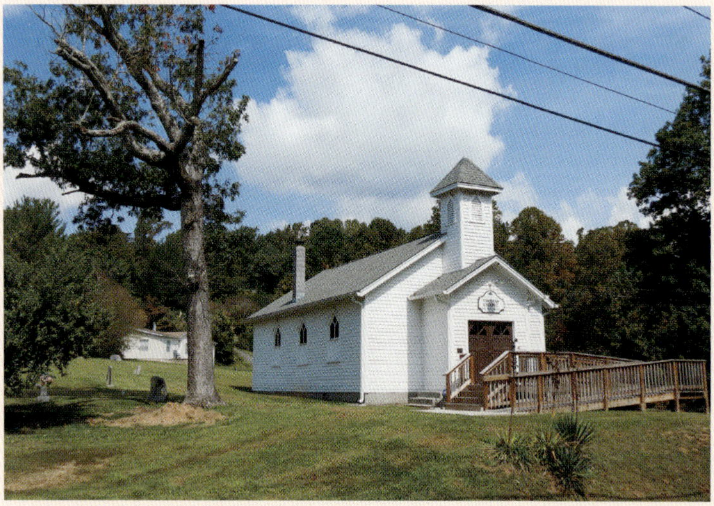

In 1892, Miles and Martha Stepp donated a log church building, Tom's Chapel—possibly the first church in Black Mountain for free African Americans—to the church's trustees. Named after two of the first founders, Tom Pertiller and Thomas Daugherty, it was later renamed the Original Thomas Chapel AME Zion Church. It was the center of religious and social life for the black community, and both Methodists and Baptists worshiped in the church until about 1910, when Mills Chapel Baptist Church was constructed. Though there are no records from the second Thomas Chapel building, the third building, which still stands and is pictured above, was erected in 1922. The congregation now meets on West College Street. In 2006, Dot Jones and Debora Hamilton Palmer, descendants of the founders, set about restoring the old church, which is now listed in the National Register of Historic Places. Below, churchgoers pose in front of what is believed to be the third Thomas Chapel building.

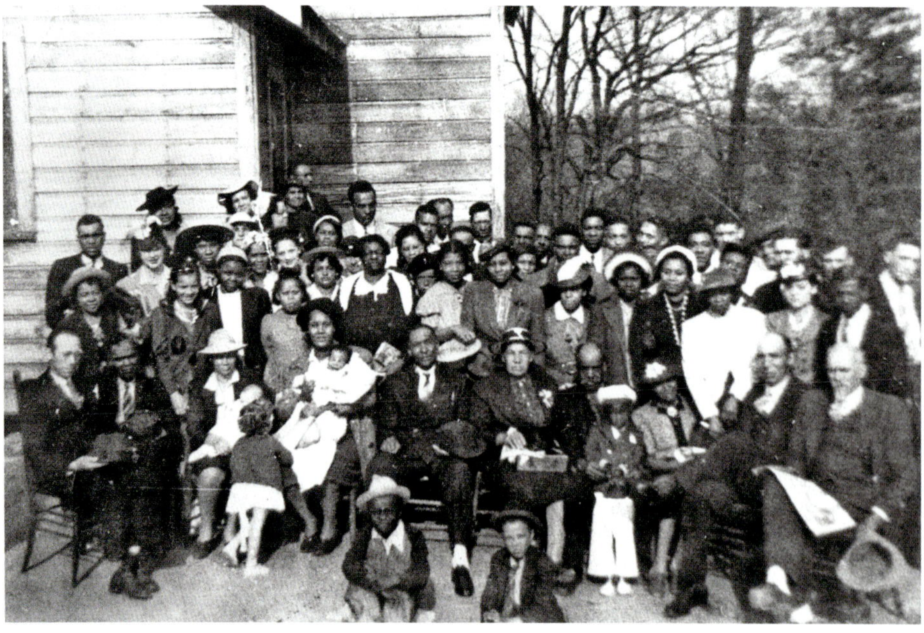

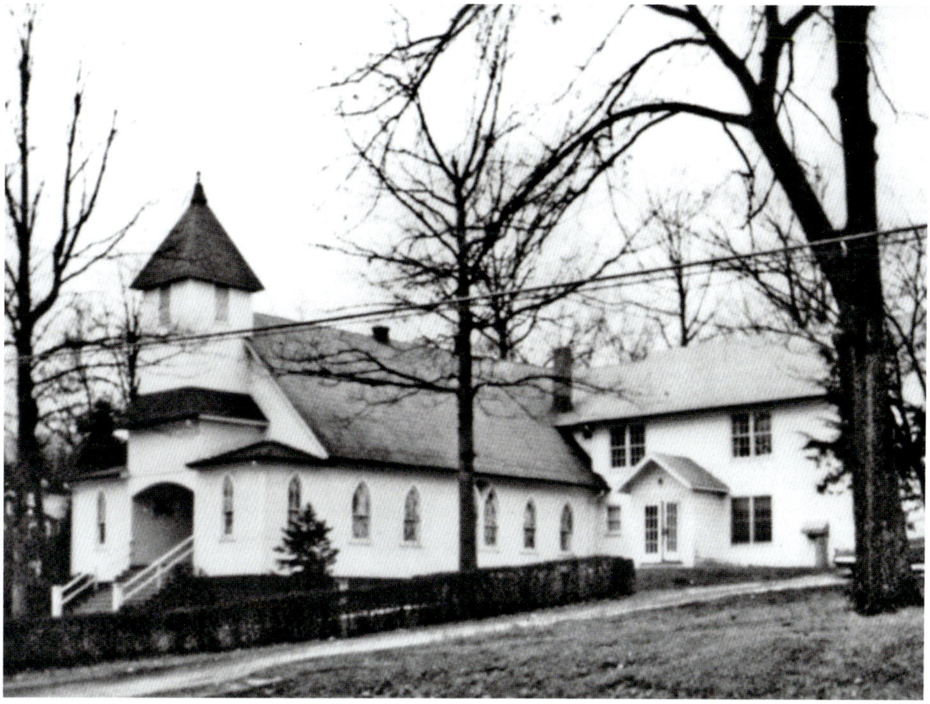

In 1908, there was no Presbyterian church in Black Mountain, so a small group met in Montreat to worship. Thirteen members chartered Black Mountain Presbyterian Church on May 17, 1908. For many years, they met in the Methodist church on State Street. The first church building was erected on Montreat Road in 1913 with pastel stained-glass windows. In 1919 and 1948, new additions were constructed. The town's first library was housed in the rear of the church from 1922 to 1923. In 1954, the church acquired additional adjoining property, and on March 30, 1958, the current sanctuary was open for worship. A new educational wing was built in 1984.

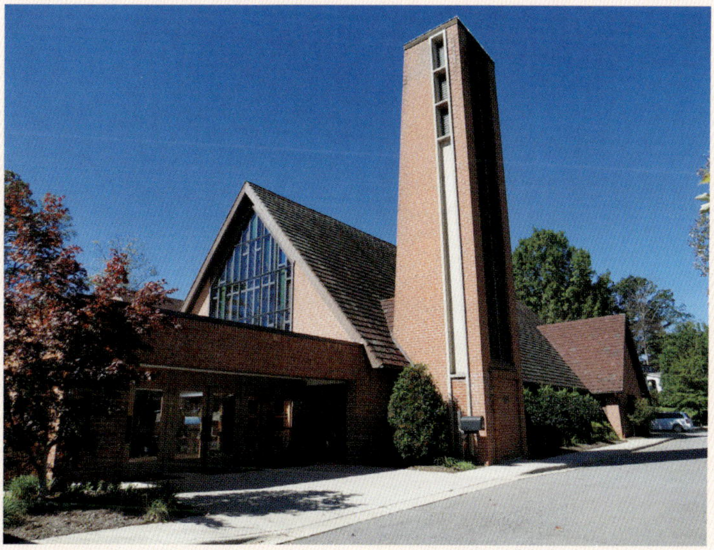

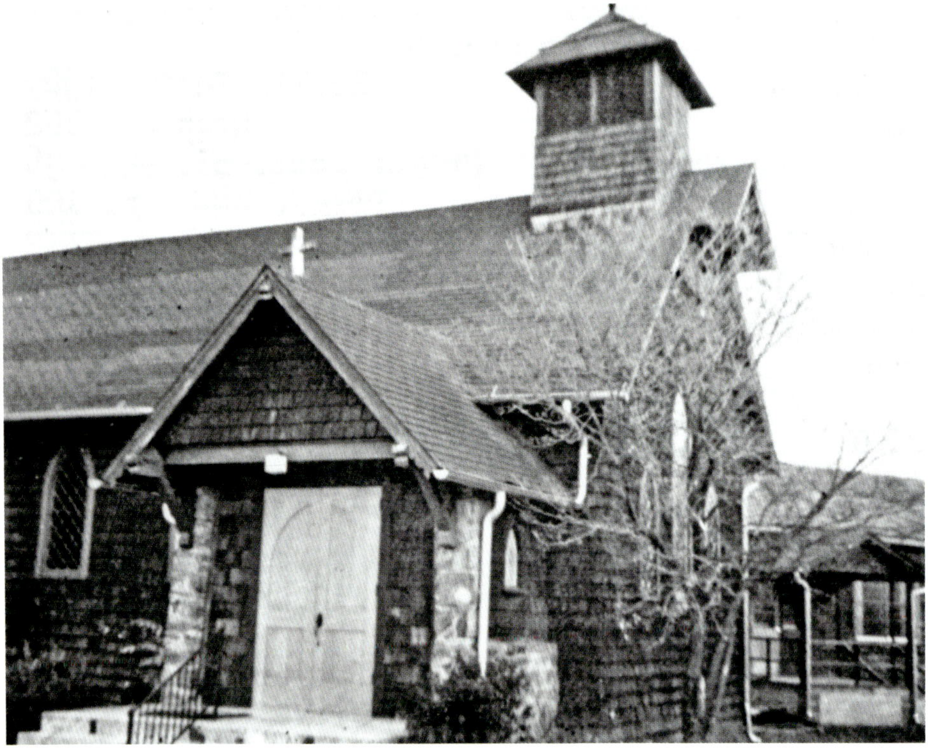

From 1907 to 1910, Episcopalians held services first in the home of a local Presbyterian, then in the Methodist church, and finally in the Black Mountain Inn before the St. James Mission was established in 1911. The cornerstone for the church on Vance Avenue was laid on July 25, 1912, and the first service was held in the unfinished building in 1917. In 1956, St. James became a parish of the Diocese of Western North Carolina. Parishioners continued to worship in the building until 1994, when a new building was completed at the corner of State Street and Cragmont Road. The church is well known for its numerous stained-glass windows, the first of which was installed in the original building in 1921 and moved, along with 15 others, to the new building in the early 1990s.

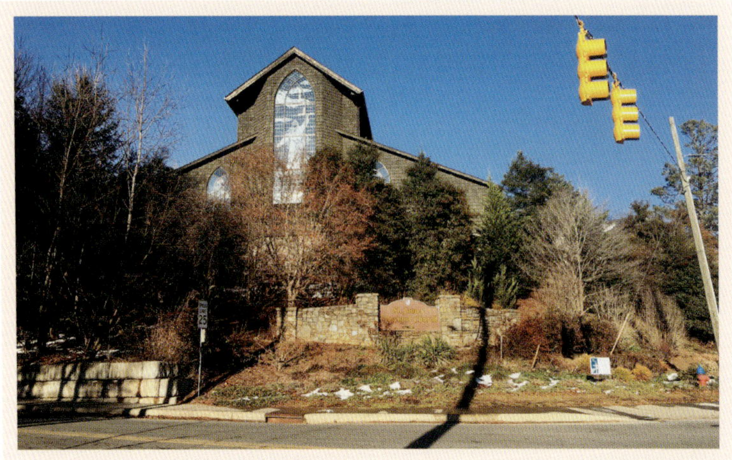

CHAPTER 6

No Place Like Home

Estates and Recreation

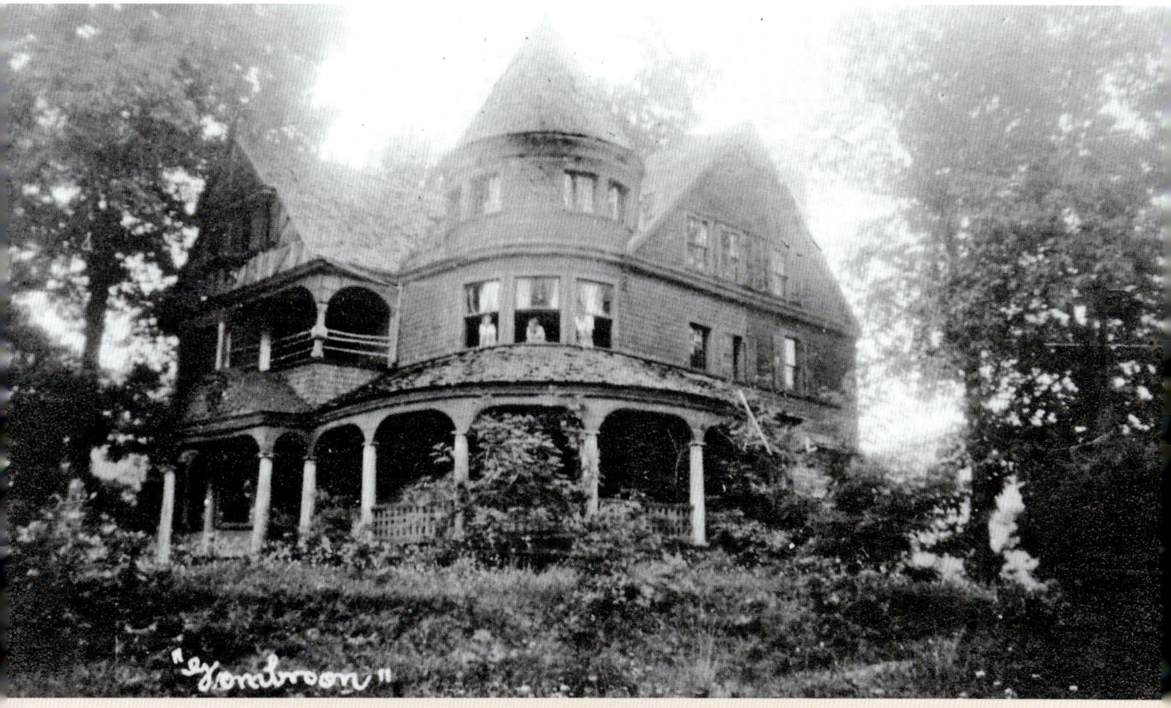

In 1883, Sen. Zebulon Baird Vance and his second wife, Florence S. Martin, selected a site for a summer home in the North Fork Valley. They built the home using almost entirely locally sourced materials and local labor. Calling the home Gombroon—chosen by Florence and meaning "an imaginary empire"—the Vances summered there until Zeb's death in 1894. On September 12, 1936, the vacant Gombroon burned to the ground from a reported lightning strike, though some suspected arson. The rocky ruins of the home, accompanying structures, and the heart-shaped fountain Zeb built for Florence still lie in the North Fork Valley, now home to Asheville's closed watershed.

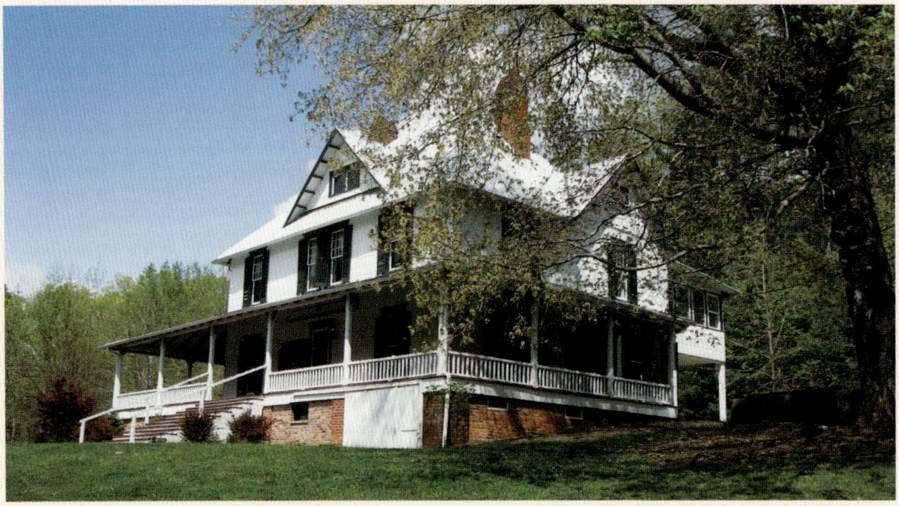

Still standing, the Vance House, pictured in the early 1900s Gertrude Sprague photograph below, was designed by Asheville architect Allen Melton around 1894 as a summer home for Kate and Charles Noel Vance, son of Zeb Vance. Like the Vances, many visitors to this popular travel destination constructed permanent summer homes that they would return to annually. The home is a rare example of a Queen Anne–style summer house in town. The property was listed in the National Register of Historic Places in 2016. (Now photograph by Jill Jones.)

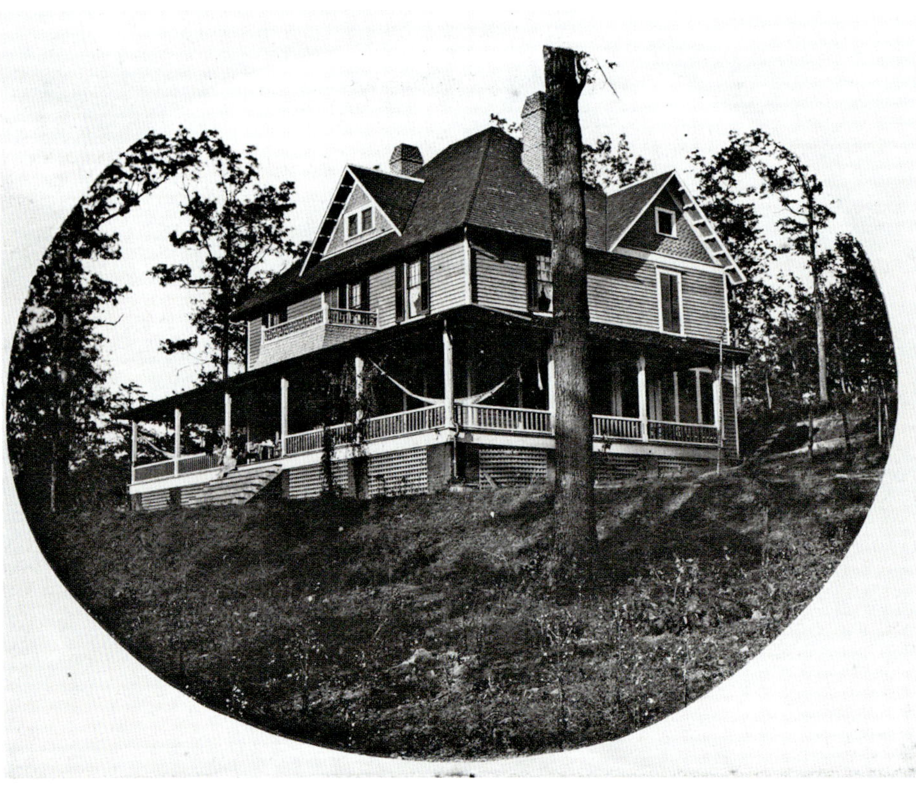

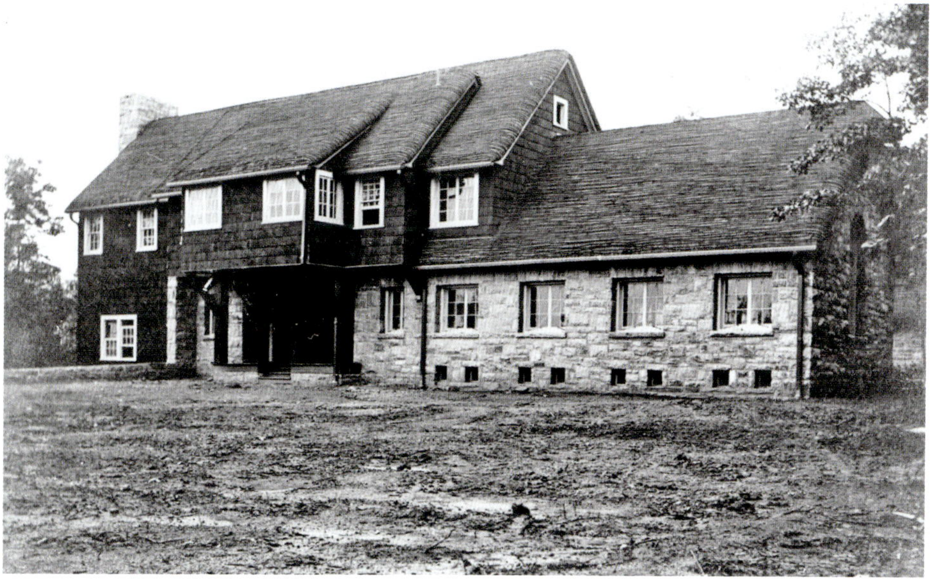

In-the-Oaks, a 24,000-square-foot Tudor-style country manor house, was built in the early 1920s for Franklin Silas Terry, the first vice president of General Electric, and his second wife—and first cousin—Lillian Estelle Slocomb Emerson. The manor boasts an indoor swimming pool, bowling alleys, and a wine cellar. Frank E. Wallis, who worked with Richard M. Hunt in New York, designed In-the-Oaks, and Richard Sharp Smith, Biltmore's supervising architect, was hired to design the recreation wing in 1923. The 80-acre property included a three-hole golf course, putting green, stables, and an extensive natural landscape designed by Frederick Law Olmsted. After Lillian's death in 1954, the estate was donated to the Episcopal Diocese as a retreat center. Montreat College purchased the property in 2001 for its Black Mountain campus. (Now photograph by Craig Cooley.)

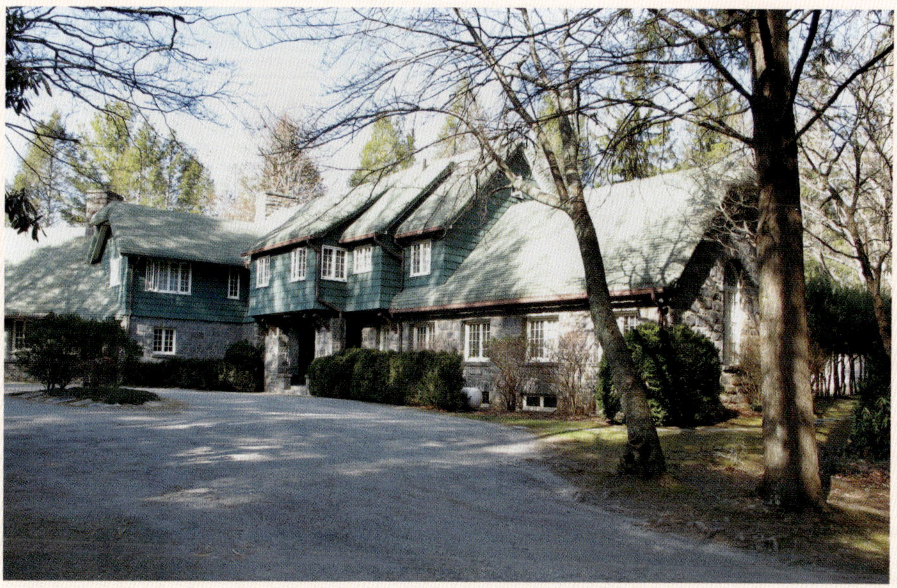

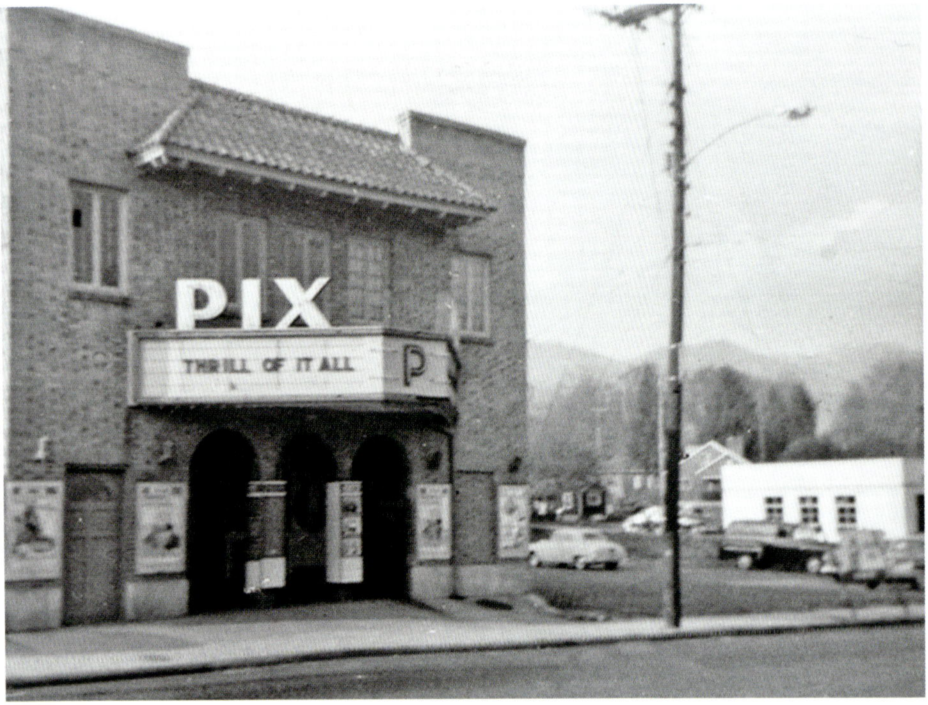

The c. 1963 photograph above shows Black Mountain's Pix Theatre. In 1924, Lee A. Hiltz built the New Theatre in the location of the present-day Town Square parking lot. Hiltz managed the theater until his death in 1945. In 1946, his wife, Bertha Nell Crawford Hiltz, sold the theater to her son Alfred J. "Laddie" Terrell Jr. and his wife, Harriette. In 1948, the Terrells leased the theater to H.D. Hearn for a term of 10 years. At this time, the name changed to the Pix Theatre. The theater closed in the 1960s, and the Terrells sold the property in 1971. To the west was a miniature golf course in the early 1930s.

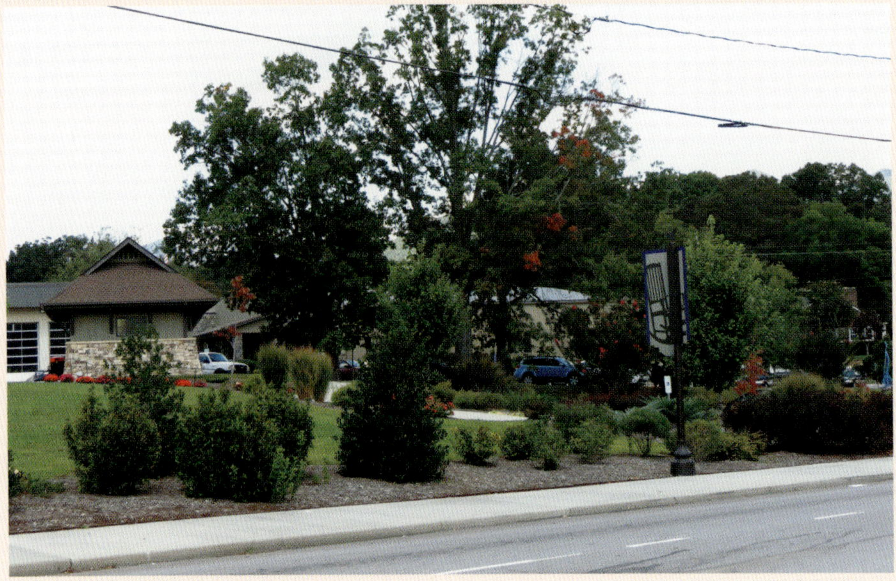

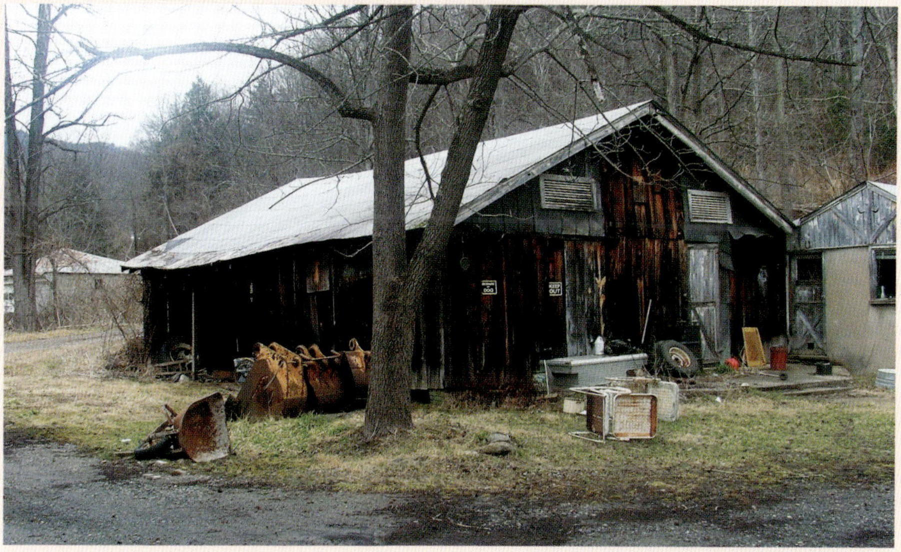

Horace Chamber Rutherford built Roseland Gardens around 1920 as a social gathering place for his friends and neighbors when segregation prohibited the black community from patronizing area restaurants, bars, pools, lakes, theaters, and music venues. The main building at Roseland Gardens provided a large open space, seen in the c. 1950 photograph below, with a wooden dance floor, stage, and movie theater. Patrons from across the region regularly made their way up the narrow dirt road to Brookside, at the intersection of Flat Creek and Padgettown Roads, until the venue closed in 1976. The original building can be seen in the 2006 photograph above by Don Talley. The building has now been demolished.

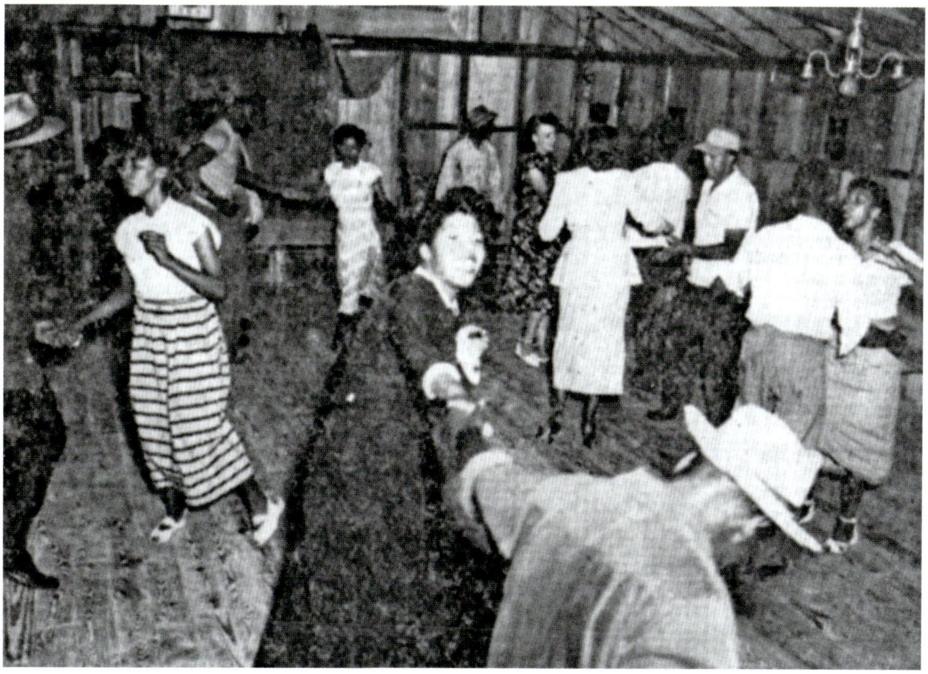

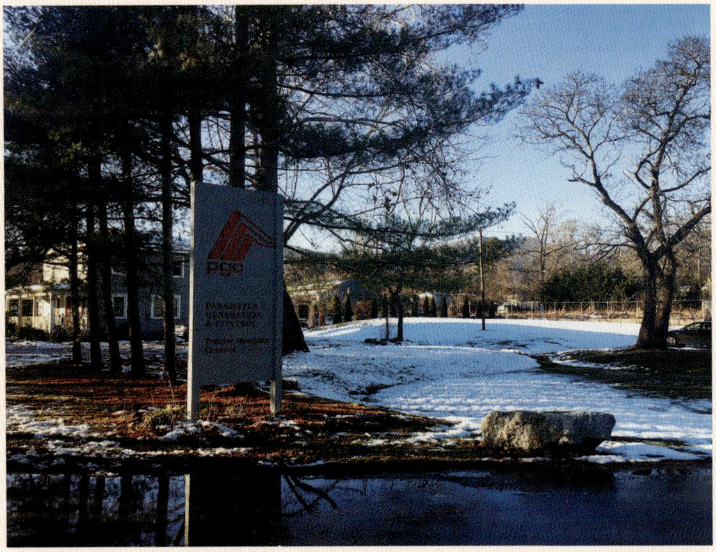

In 1937, Roy S. Campbell built Roy's Inn with a dance floor and furnished it with a soda fountain, eight booths, and a peanut vending machine. In 1938, Black Mountain College student Stephen Forbes purchased the establishment and leased it back to Campbell for just $30 a month so that students and faculty at the college would have an off-campus place to socialize. In 1940, Forbes sold the property to Joe Lance, who managed Roy's with his wife. New managers changed the name from Roy's Inn to the Brown Derby Tavern in 1944. In 1946, Raymond R. Peek and his wife, Selina, opened Peek's Place in the building, alternately known as Peek's Tavern and Ada's The Brown Derby. Raymond was also proprietor of the Farmer's Ball Square Dances on Farm School Road.

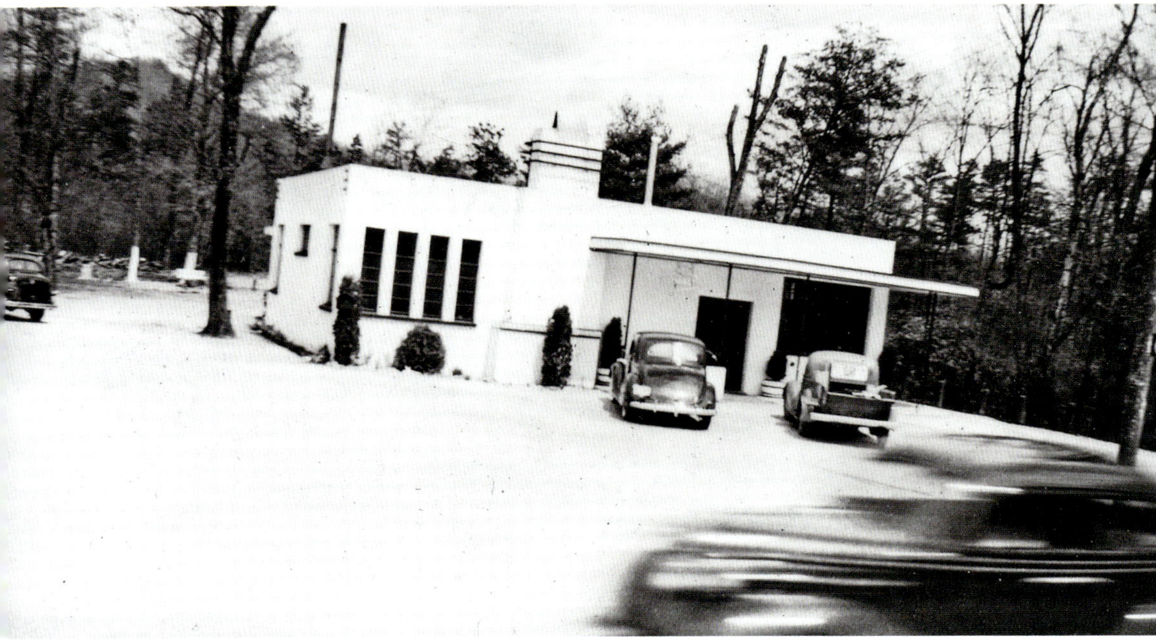

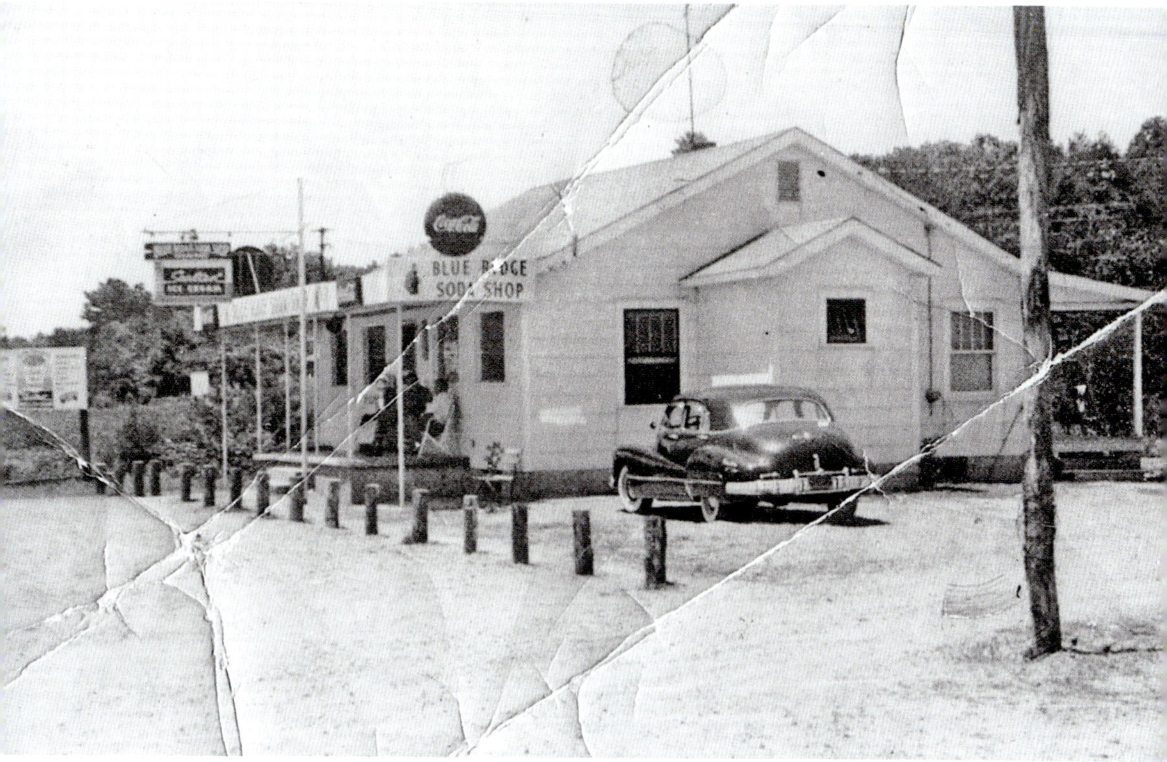

Willard Browning ran the Blue Ridge Soda Shop and restaurant next door to his grocery (page 57). Here patrons could get sodas, milkshakes, hamburgers, and other fast food from Browning and his wife, Flossie. After school, students from Owen High School would gather for milkshakes and to play the Wurlitzer jukebox. The building moved to Richardson Boulevard, across from the post office, and became home to Don's Family Restaurant, run by Don and Martha Gallion. It now contains office space.

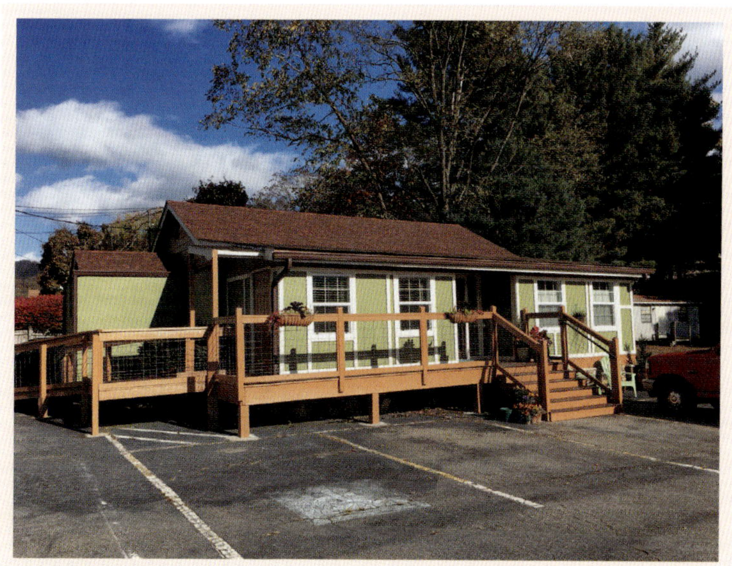

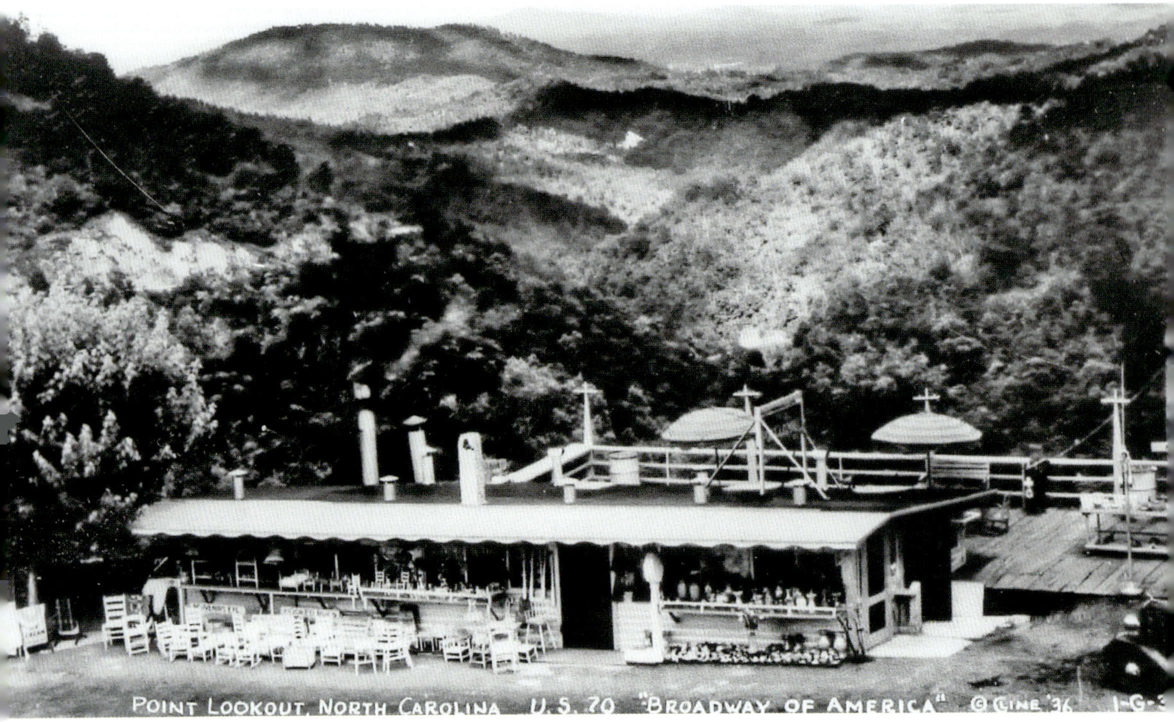

Point Lookout, on Old US 70 between Ridgecrest and Old Fort, is pictured in the 1936 postcard above. During Point Lookout's heyday in the 1920s–1940s, US 70 was the major thoroughfare for tourists traveling across the state. This section of the road was steep and winding. Point Lookout, besides having a magnificent view of Royal Gorge, also provided motorists a place to stop and rest their engines and brakes. In the 1930s, H.A. Ragle of Old Fort added a retail shop, gas station, and motel. This steep section of road was closed in 1968, and in 2008, the Point Lookout Trail opened. Though Point Lookout's structures are gone, the view of Royal Gorge remains, as seen in the 2011 photograph by Joe Standaert below.

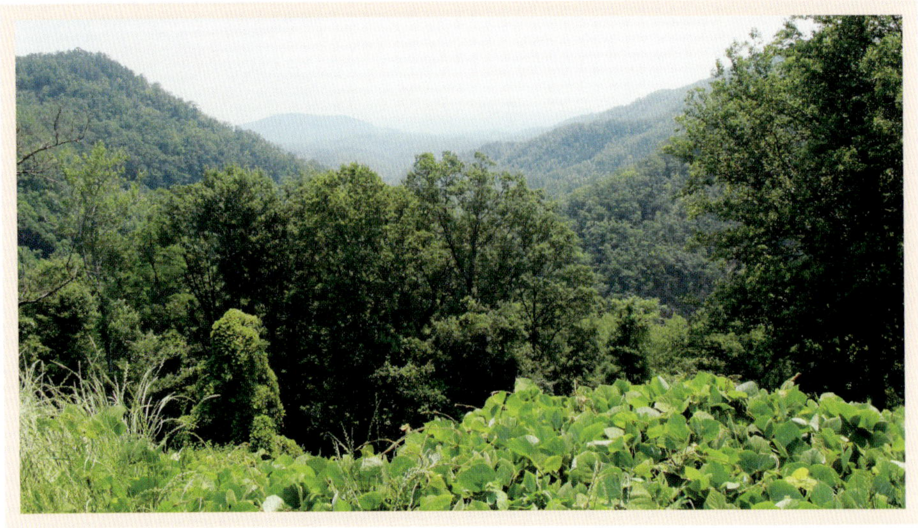

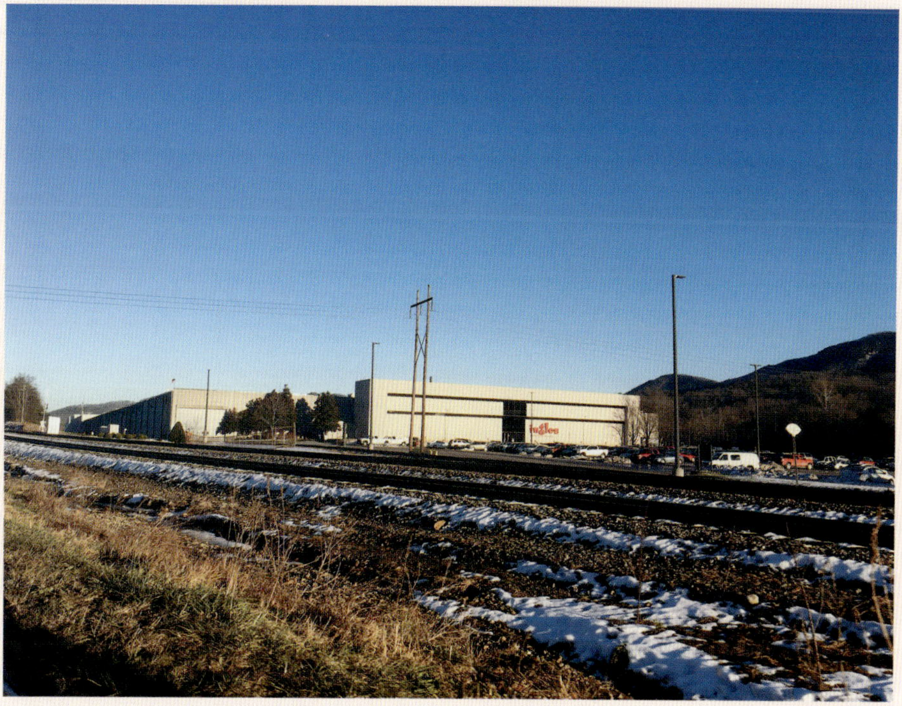

As early as November 1931, the Black Mountain Airport was operating with a temporary runway, and it drew large crowds by hosting flying stunts—wingwalkers and parachute jumpers. Eventually the airport would have two runways, one over a mile long. After World War II, William C. "Red" Nichols purchased the airport, which had fallen into disrepair. In 1946, he started Nichols Flying Service, a school and business transporting passengers to the Asheville-Hendersonville Airport. In 1959, Nichols leased the land to Blue Ridge Broadcasting for its radio studio with the stipulation it would not interfere with the runway, and he sold it to the broadcaster outright in 1961. In 2007, the land was sold to the Ingles grocery store chain for a large warehouse.

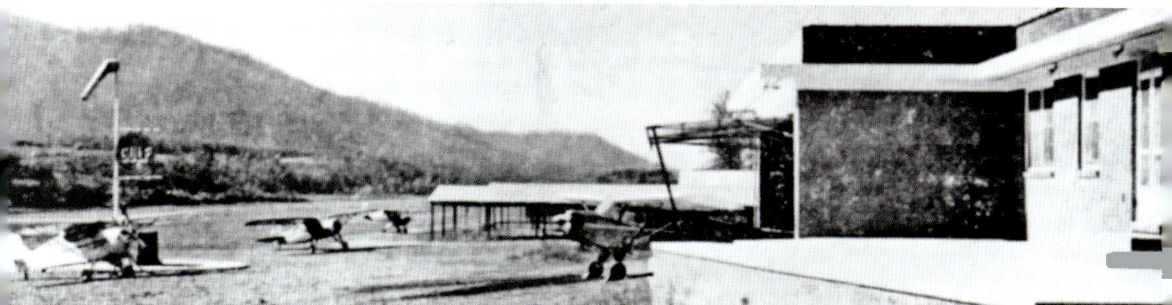

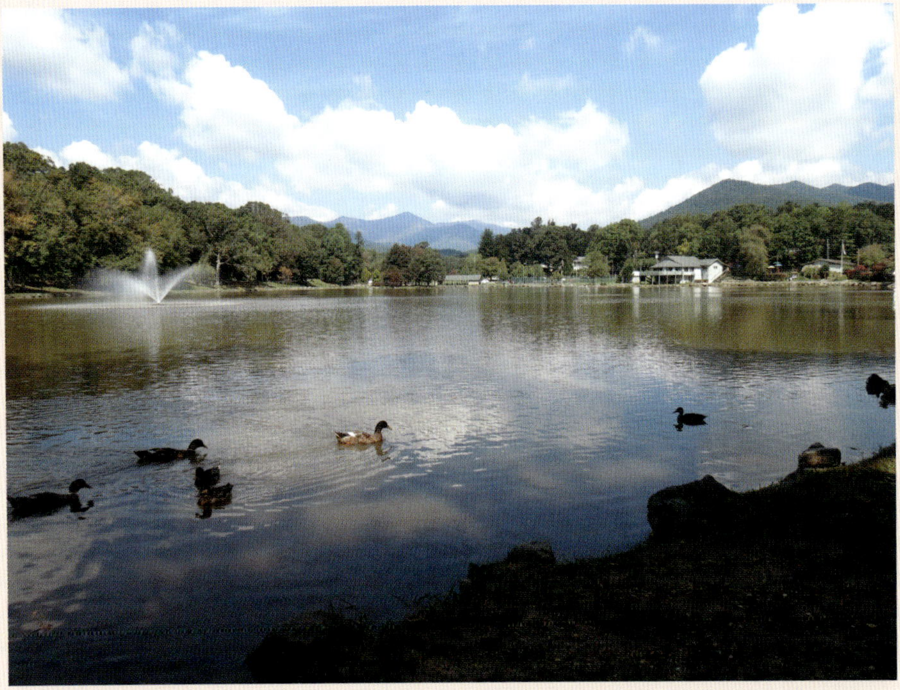

As early as 1913, plans for Lake Tomahawk were under consideration as part of the Methodist colony that was to be built just northwest of town. When the colony's plans fell through, the town, aided by funds from the Civil Works Administration and later the Federal Emergency Relief Administration (FERA), began work on a recreation center on the site. On Labor Day weekend 1934, the town officially opened Lake Tomahawk and the Community House with a day of water sports, including speedboat racing. In 1938, the lake closed to swimmers due to water quality issues, and a pool was constructed.

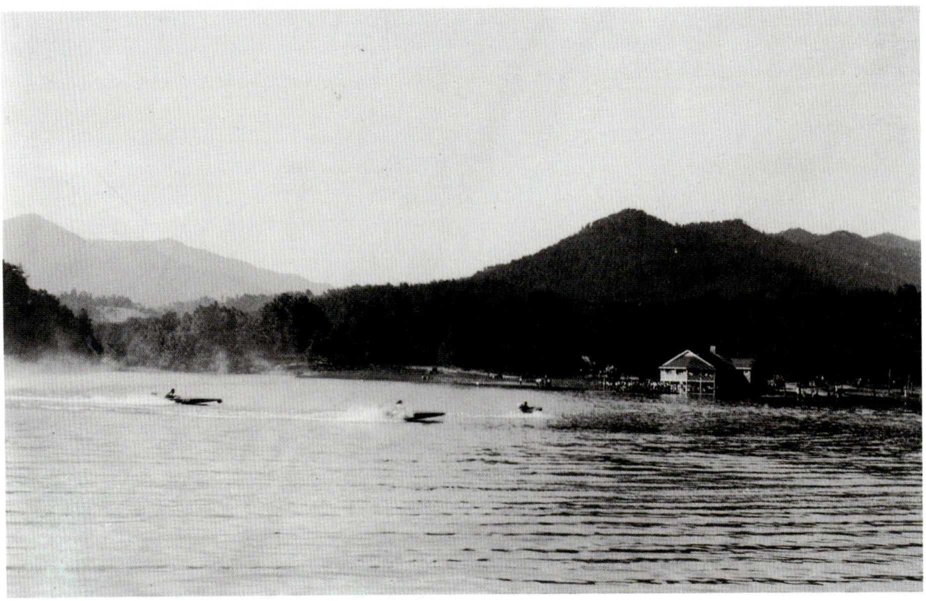

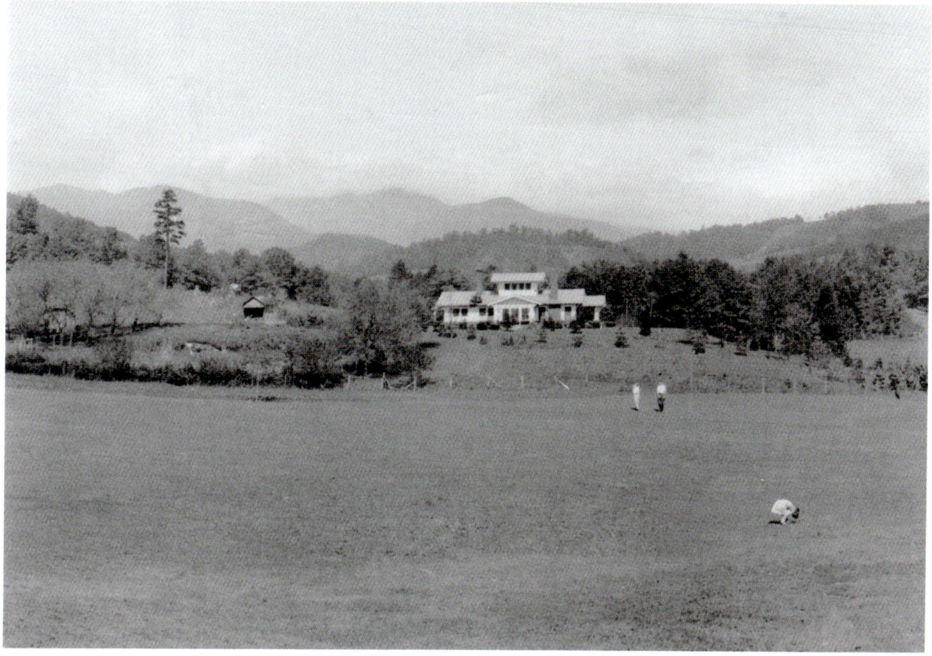

The 1926 Gragg Studio photograph above shows the Rome and Essie Garland home. Its foundation was used to build the Black Mountain golf course clubhouse. In 1933, Black Mountain planned to extend and rebuild its 1920s-era 18-acre golf course as part of the Lake Tomahawk recreation center. Using FERA and Works Progress Administration funds, the new nine-hole course was in operation by the summer of 1936. In 1937, the town banned cattle grazing on the golf course. With the help of Rev. Billy Graham, an avid golfer, the North Fork Dairy, which adjoined the course, was purchased in 1963 to expand the course to the 18 holes it is today. On May 15, 1964, the back nine was dedicated, with Graham taking the first shot off No. 10.

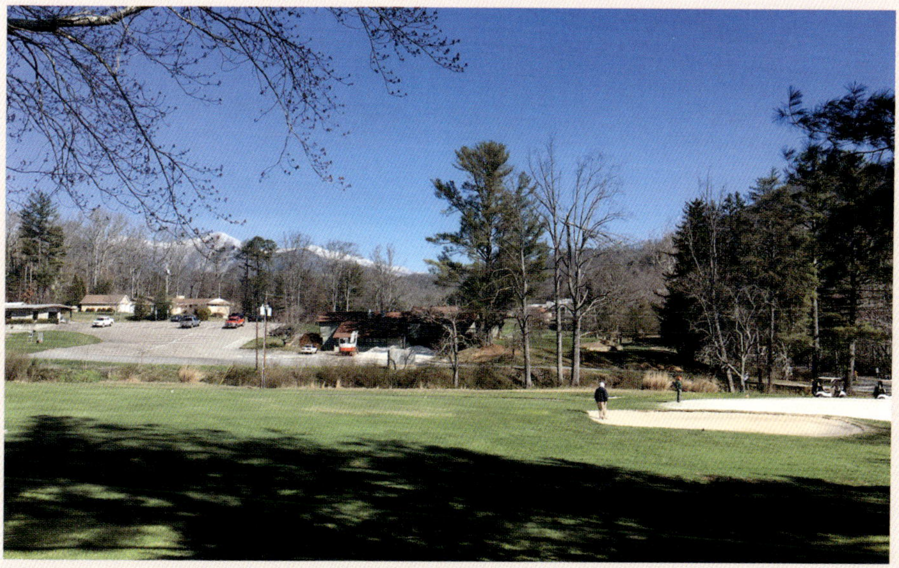

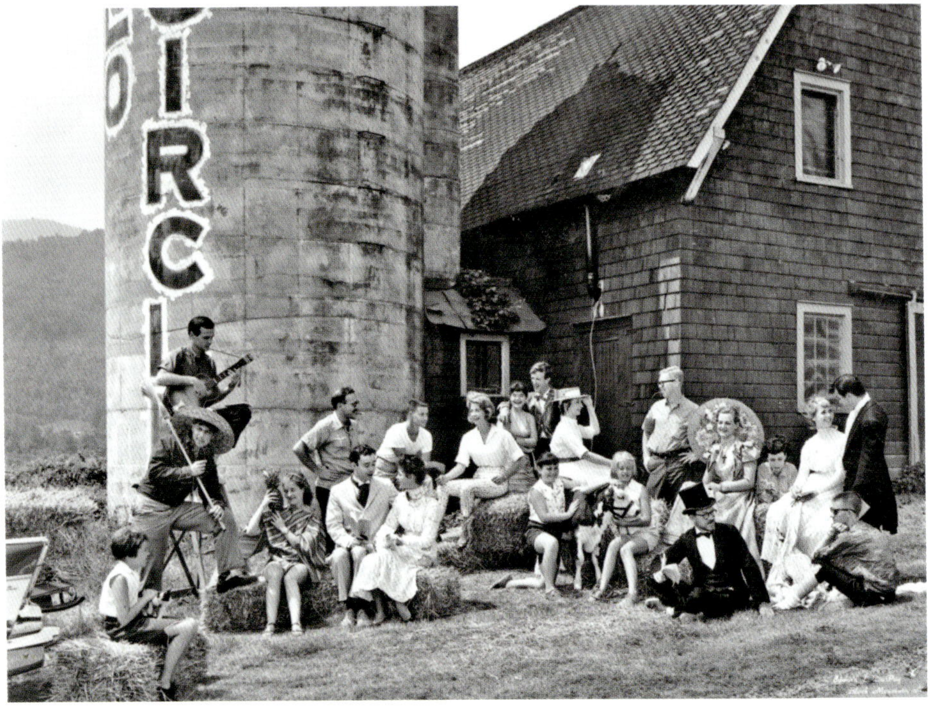

The cast and crew of a production at Silo Circle Theatre is pictured above around 1960. Between 1958 and 1961, the Broadway-style theater operated during the summer months. The idea was first proposed by young actors and producers Tinka Crawford, Norman Kean, and Dale Meador. The company bought and renovated a cattle barn that had been part of the state test farm, adding lights, a stage, and seating areas. The company put on seven shows each summer, selling tickets for $2 each or season passes for a discounted rate. It closed due to financial difficulties. Owen Pool was built near the former site of the theater.

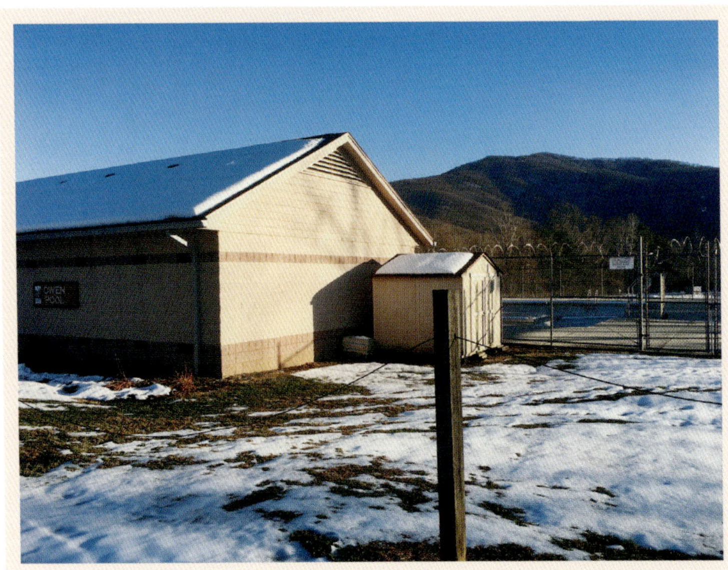

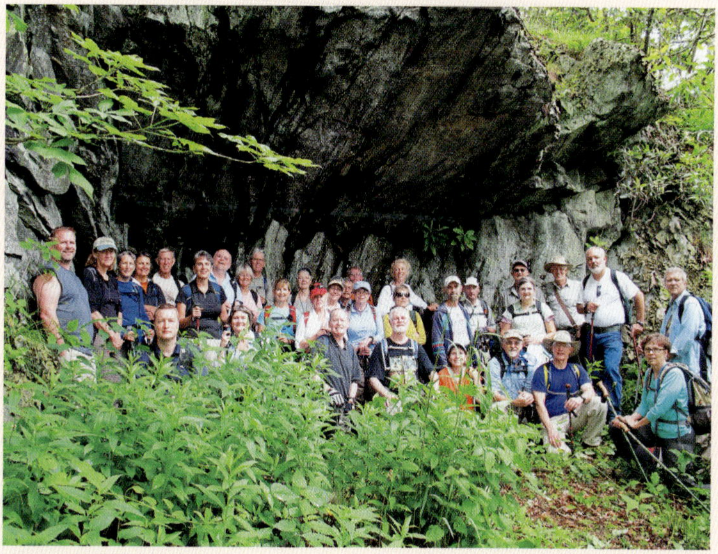

Hiking has been a favorite pastime of locals and visitors to Black Mountain for centuries. In the early 1900 Gertrude Sprague image below, an unidentified hiker rests beneath the famous camp rock near Mount Mitchell. In the present-day photograph above by Swannanoa Valley Museum hike leader Joe Standaert, a group of Swannanoa Rim Explorer Hike Series hikers poses under a camp rock between Rocky Knob and Graybeard Mountain on the Museum's Pinnacle of the Blue Ridge hike.

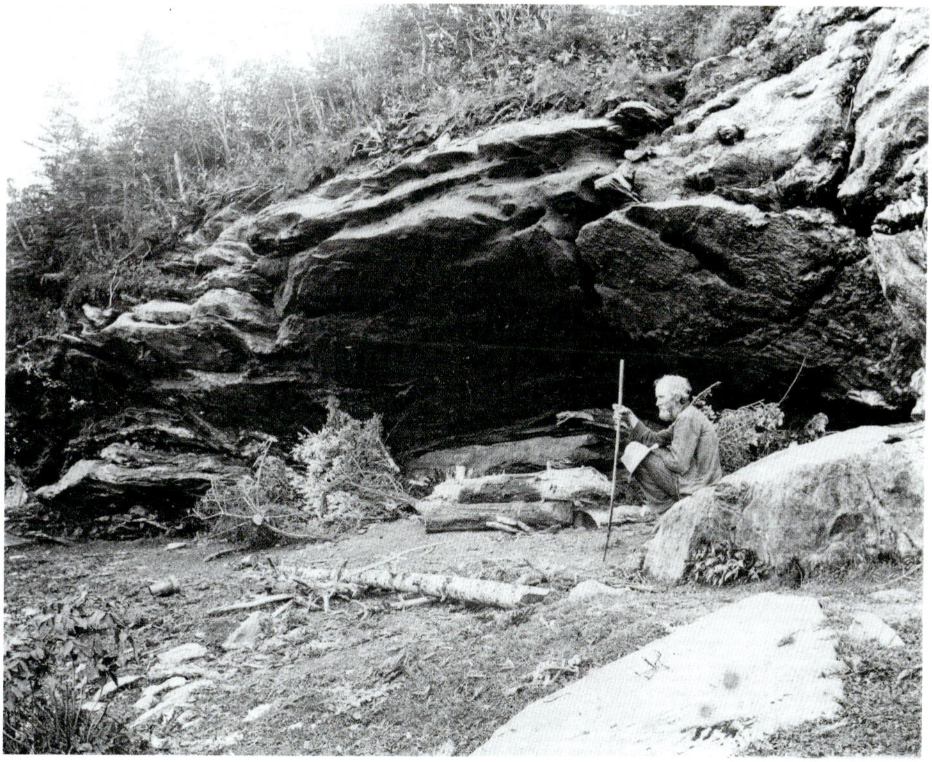